PUSKÁS

PUSKÁS

Madrid, The Magyars and the Amazing Adventures
of the World's Greatest Goalscorer

GYÖRGY SZÖLLŐSI

Translated from the Hungarian by Andrew Clark and
Matthew Watson-Broughton with special thanks to Márton Dinnyés

First published in Hungary by Ringier/Mediaworks
Second impression 2016

All images courtesy of the Puskás Institute and PUSKAS.COM

Freight Books
49-53 Virginia Street
Glasgow, G1 1TS
www.freightbooks.co.uk

A CIP catalogue reference for this book is available
from the British Library

ISBN: 978-1-910449-45-5

the publisher acknowledges investment from
Creative Scotland toward the publication of this book

Typeset by Freight in Plantin MT
Printed and bound by Hussar Books, Poland

'Love is seeing someone,
just as God sees all of us.'

FOREWORD

Sir Alex Ferguson

I was a young boy when Ferenc Puskás burst onto the scene unexpectedly and I believe therein lies the distinction of how true greatness is defined. The great players do things that you don't expect, so when I dodged school on that Wednesday afternoon in 1953 to watch the England v Hungary match on TV at a misty Wembley, no one expected what we were about to witness: a new way of playing football and, of course, the great goal when Ferenc pulled the ball back as the England captain, Billy Wright, slid in to tackle but ended up among the photographers behind the goal-line. It was nothing short of breathtaking.

One has to think of the impact that had on a 12-year-old kid in Glasgow. After the game I was out in the back court practising that pull-back with my left foot and banging the ball into an empty goal. It was a football revolution. Teams started copying the way Hungary played, with the Hidegkuti role of a player dropping deep to link the play and the inside-forwards – like Puskás and Kocsis – becoming the strikers.

That next summer they were cruelly denied the greatest prize when West Germany came from 2-0 down to beat Hungary in the World Cup final in Switzerland, although one has to say that an injury to Puskás earlier in the tournament cost them the game. The Hungary fever carried on and once more there was great excitement and anticipation in Scotland when several of the Hungarian players turned up at the British Embassy looking for asylum after the Uprising in their homeland in 1956. The Scottish papers were almost in convulsions – one day Puskás was signing for Celtic, the next day it was Rangers. However, as we now know, it was Spain and Real Madrid who were able to persuade him to go there and win three European Cups as part of the club's golden era.

He is the only player to score four goals in a final – in 1960 at Hampden in their 7-3 win over Eintracht Frankfurt. I was a player at Queen's Park, the Scottish club who play their home games at the national stadium, and I was able to get a ticket for the enclosure to witness the greatest final of all time.

When Madrid eventually lost a final it was to Benfica after extra time, in 1962, but once again Puskás left his mark by scoring a hat-trick in a 5-3 defeat. Can you imagine scoring three goals in the European Cup final and losing!

I was fortunate to have seen him play and he was without question one of the greatest players of all time. It was an honour to have met his wife Erzsébet recently when I visited Hungary and I was impressed at how humble she was. Maybe his greatness spread everywhere.

Alex Ferguson

Sir Alex Ferguson CBE

INTRODUCTION
The Legacy

Today the legacy of Ferenc Puskás is perhaps most visible once a year, at the FIFA Player of the Year gala, when the award bearing his name is given for the goal of the year. Winners have included Cristiano Ronaldo, Neymar and Zlatan Ibrahimovic – what better endorsement for the award than in 2013, seeing the childish excitement in Zlatan, the coolest man on the planet, as he waited to see if he had won for his extraordinary overhead kick against England.

That the award exists is down to a group of Puskás fans which includes myself, Erzsébet Puskás, the widow of the great footballer, and Sepp Blatter, the president of FIFA.

At the 2007 UEFA Congress in Dusseldorf, Ferenc Puskás was posthumously awarded UEFA's highest accolade, the Order of Merit in Emerald. In my role as one of the leaders of the Puskás Academy and a close friend of the family, I accompanied Erzsébet to the ceremony. When Erzsébet was invited to meet Blatter, she slipped him an envelope, which contained a proposal for the Puskás Award.

At that point, the proposal by another Puskás fan, Dr István Csorba, was to adapt the Golden Shoe award with more balanced evaluations of the goals scored globally each year in order to better reward the greatest goalscorer in world football that year, and to name the new award after Puskás. At the ceremony, we had the chance to speak to Blatter about it, who responded positively.

What happened next changed football history. Instead of adapting the Golden Shoe, Blatter proposed a new 'goal of the year' award, to be decided by a public vote.

More time passed and just as it seemed as if it would be lost in a maze of bureaucracy, I buttonholed Blatter in his hotel after the 2008 Champions League final in Moscow, won by Manchester United against Chelsea.

"We will do it," he told me emphatically. By this point, we had garnered substantial support. Hungarian athletes, politicians, scientists and artists all wrote letters imploring FIFA to follow through on the proposal.

Eventually Blatter himself came to Hungary to personally sign the contract and visit the Puskás Academy. The official announcement was made on October 20, 2009, and in December of that year the first Puskás Award was awarded to Ronaldo by Erzsébet in Zurich. It was the one and only time Erzsébet has presented the award.

Ronaldo's goal was a worthy first winner, a 40-yard rocket for Manchester United against FC Porto in the Champions League, seeing off strikes from Fernando Torres, Andrés Iniesta and Michael Essien on the shortlist.

The key figure in making it all happen was Blatter. As well as being a supporter of the great Real Madrid team of the 1950s and early 60s, the FIFA president was in the stands at the World Cup final in 1954, when Hungary lost to West Germany. Little did we know when we set out on this path that the head of football's governing body was a bona fide Puskás fan.

Of course, Blatter is not alone in that.

It was 1986. I was nine years old and dressed in football kit at a school fancy-dress gala in Budapest. I was singing a popular song with 10 of my classmates about Hungary's great 6-3 victory over England in 1953. It was the first time I had heard the great names of the Magical Magyars.

That in itself was no surprise. Hungary's 'Golden Team' – *Aranycsapat* in Hungarian – was officially 'forgotten' by the communist regime after the 1956 revolution, when some of the best players such as Puskás, Czibor and Kocsis went into exile. After this experience, I asked my father again and again about the great team and the legendary players. I also read the books which were allowed to be published on the subject – mainly written after 1981, when Puskás came home by official invitation for the first time following his exile, 25 years earlier.

I was a university student studying journalism when the family of another student asked me to write a book about their uncle, a famous footballer who had returned home from Spain after many years. They were the Czibors. It was unbelievable – I was 19 and visited Zoltán Czibor, the great former Hungary and FC Barcelona player, every week in his home town of Komárom, recording interviews, studying photos and hearing stories about his miraculous career. He died before we finished our work together, but my book was published in the same year, 1997, by a publisher who paid for my university studies as the honorarium.

A year after my book was published, I started work at the daily sports newspaper *Nemzeti Sport*. My particular area of responsibility was to write about historical football issues. The best-known journalists wrote about the current football players in Hungary but I was very happy to meet former players who represented a much higher level of football. I was invited to their anniversaries and accompanied them to some events abroad.

Ferenc Puskás, the most popular and best-known Hungarian footballer, attended my first book presentation and we met more and more often at gatherings and football matches. Through this work, and later as press officer for the Hungarian FA, I travelled with Puskás many times, and came to feel accepted by him. We received daily letters from all over the world from fans asking for autographs or photos, even as Puskás became gravely ill.

Puskás was visited in hospital every day by his wife, Erzsébet, who helped me a great deal in the production of this book. With her guidance I researched in Madrid, Athens and Brussels, collecting photos from Canada and Australia. It was like a dream, following in the footsteps of Puskás.

Three months before his death, Erzsébet asked me to represent Puskás at the ceremony of the Golden Foot award in Monaco where he was due to receive an award at the same time as Ronaldo, Raymond Kopa, Zico, Just Fontaine, Javier Zanetti and Alcides Ghiggia. So, in August 2006, I stood on stage with the Golden Foot award alongside these superstars in order to represent the great Ferenc Puskás.

This book has changed my life. When Puskás died in November 2006 I became the spokesman for and a member of the farewell committee led by Pál Schmitt, the president of the Hungarian Olympic Committee (and later President of Hungary). It was an unforgettable ceremony with the greatest personalities of the football world present.

The rights for my book were bought by FilmPlus in 2006 who produced a documentary, 'Puskás Hungary', which was awarded the best documentary film of the year prize in Hungary in 2009 and the best documentary film of the Valladolid Film Festival in 2010.

In 2006, I acted as mediator between Viktor Orbán, the

current Hungarian Prime Minster, and the Puskás family, when Orbán's foundation began to build the Ferenc Puskás Football Academy, a sport school and football centre near Budapest. It is now the biggest and best equipped football centre in Central Europe and I have worked for the institution since the beginning. Today I am the director of the Puskás Institute which publishes the Hungarian edition of FourFourTwo magazine under my editorship and which is continuously developing a museum, archive, library and is home to the definitive collection of photos and films from Hungarian football history.

The basis of our collection has come directly from Puskás' family as his daughter Anikó (who died in 2011) decided to give to the Puskás Academy all of her father's trophies and memorabilia. This huge collection came home from Spain in 2009 in 20 giant metal boxes and is why we can now present to our visitors the Olympic gold medal, the World Cup silver medal, the 'Pichichi' Primera Liga top goalscorer trophies, the football boots and the Real Madrid shirt of Puskás, besides many other fantastic items.

It is also through the generosity of the Puskás family that we have the stories on these pages.

György Szöllősi, Felcsút, 2015

PROLOGUE
The man in Room 602

They had scored goals in European Cup finals, they had stunned a Wembley crowd. They had been the instruments of a genius that had led many to proclaim him the greatest footballer in the world. They now slid inside a pair of simple shoes that were at least five sizes too big.

Ferenc Puskás was in his room at the Kútvölgyi hospital, near Budapest. He was ill, disorientated. The player who could confound a defence with a shimmy, a drag-back with a piece of thinking so sharp that it would wound, the personality who could converse in a range of languages, had been brutally diminished by a form of cerebral sclerosis.

The supreme footballer, a power who had created memories for a generation and beyond, now struggled to remember, to think lucidly.

His carer came into his room, his large feet slapping on the floor, He asked Puskás why he was wearing his shoes. Puskás just smiled: "They are really good."

Ferenc Puskás, the greatest Hungarian, the hero of Bernabéu, the leader of a football revolution that culminated in massacres of the England national side of the 1950s, was to spend his last six years in this room.

He had been forced into exile from Hungary and travelled the world, living on his wits and his physical genius. His life was now spent in Room 602. He seemed happy to watch football on television, though he was patient and tolerant when the decoder that allowed him to access Real Madrid TV was regularly stolen by a fellow patient who suffered from a form of kleptomania.

He flicked through Nemzeti Sport, the Hungarian sports daily that was delivered every day. No one knew how much he took in. Puskás did not say.

His communication was limited, often baffling. His wife remembered how his illness started: "He got up after his afternoon siesta and didn't know if it was evening or morning. At first he had trouble with counting. Before this he could count brilliantly, he added up and took away all sorts of amounts within moments. After that, one time it didn't come out. He didn't understand it. He counted it again and again but it didn't come out."

This is how it began. In 1995, Puskás fell ill. It took him more than a decade to succumb to an illness that first saw him admitted to what was called, crudely and cruelly, 'the loony bin of Budapest', before he was transferred to the Kútvölgyi.

He died in 2006, aged 79, in a room which was comfortable but humble: a bed, a chair and a television. This room became the final destination of a pilgrimage undertaken by Sepp Blatter, the FIFA president, Alfredo Di Stéfano, Puskás' brilliant partner at Real Madrid, officials from the Spanish football association, members of the Hungarian team of the 1950s that deserves to be in any argument about the greatest side ever. A few fortunate supporters were also allowed to gaze on greatness, if they somehow won the trust of the hospital and the family.

Puskás, normally serene, would occasionally become restless. He would say to his wife: "I have to go out to the pitch." She would take him out to the corridor and the player who stood in tunnels awaiting a World Cup or European final would relax.

On other occasions, he would suddenly stop eating his lunch and stand up, saying: "The guys are waiting."

Until the end, he was fascinated by the ball. Jenő Kovács, his faithful carer, would bring the sports paper, and arrange the seat of the great man in front of the television. But he also had a duty that he considered unbelievable, almost sacred.

Kovács, like every Hungarian, had a devotion to Puskás that owed much to the great man's football ability but more to his place in the country's history.

Puskás had been the child prodigy whose name was whispered as a future great on street corners in Budapest. He had been the player who led the nation to the very brink of World Cup glory. He had become the exiled hero, escaping the communist dictatorship in 1956 for an uncertain future abroad. He was synonymous with the great Real Madrid side of the 1960s and became a coach who took Panathinaikos of Greece to a European Cup final.

He was, above all, a physical reminder to Hungary of past glories and historic trials. He was, too, a victim of his times who was almost certainly sentenced to death by the Hungarian government when he went into exile. Hungary, the land of his birth, would become the land of his death if he returned under communist rule.

As the grip of communism loosened and then broke, Puskás did come back, but, finally, not to a Budapest mansion, but to a hospital room. Sometimes he roamed just that little bit further.

Kovács, with a sense of unreality that never quite left him, would take Puskás by the arm, if the weather was good and the legend agreeable, and lead him outside with a ball. Occasionally, they would visit the stadium in Budapest that carries the name of Puskás. They would pass the ball around, the hospital carer and one of the greatest players ever.

Kovács would watch, his sense of astonishment never diminishing, as the old man would control the ball flawlessly, and shoot with power and innate technique.

Puskás, the man, was failing. Puskás, the footballer, was undimmed, adding to the legend that had surrounded him in life and would trail him in death.

DRAMATIS PERSONAE

Alfredo Di Stéfano: Regarded as one of the greatest footballers of all time, the Argentine was the leader of the great Real Madrid side of the 1950s and early 60s. Struck up a rapport with Puskás – whom he called 'Pancho' – on and off the field after the Hungarian joined Los Blancos in 1958

Zoltán Czibor: Team-mate of Puskás' for Honvéd and the Hungarian national team. Provided the assist for Puskás' famous drag-back goal in the Magyars' 6-3 defeat of England in 1953. Like Puskás, enjoyed a productive 'second career' in Spain, with Madrid's great rivals Barcelona

Ferenc Purczeld (Puskás senior): A former footballer with Kispest, he went on to manage Honvéd to their first league title in 1949-50. Supposedly drank 34 *fröccs* (wine spritzer) in one sitting, an achievement outweighed by nurturing Puskás junior

József Bozsik: Grew up in the same building as Puskás in Kispest, played on the same sand pitch as children and went on to become Olympic champions and World Cup runners-up together. Puskás believed Bozsik to be the best footballer of all time. Became MP before the Uprising in addition to his footballing role and returned to Hungary after the tour of 1956, eventually amassing a Hungarian record of 101 international caps

Gyula Grosics: Goalkeeper Grosics was a mainstay of the great Honvéd team and was capped 86 times for Hungary. He won Olympic gold, was in goal for the 6-3 Wembley match and selected in the 'Team of the tournament' at the 1954 World Cup

Sándor Kocsis: Prolific scorer alongside Puskás at Honvéd, he went on to strike 11 times for Hungary at the 1954 World Cup, including two hat-tricks – making him the tournament's top goalscorer. He played with Czibor at Ferencváros, Honvéd and at Barcelona, where they won La Liga and reached the final of the 1961 European Cup, both scoring in a 3-2 defeat by Benfica

Erzsébet Puskás: Married Puskás in 1950 and they were together until his death in 2006. Escaped from revolutionary Hungary in November 1956 under the cover of darkness and together the couple raised a daughter, Anikó

Emil Östreicher: Mr Fixit. Östreicher was Honvéd's financial secretary and later negotiated Puskás' surprise move to Madrid, where Östreicher subsequently became technical director

Mihály Farkas: A key figure in the communist government of Mátyás Rákosi, as Minister of National Defence from 1948 to 1953, and the point of contact for Puskás, who would lobby on behalf of athletes who fell foul of the regime

László Kubala: Kubala twice left Hungary – in 1946 to play in, and for, Czechoslovakia, and then in 1949, after the establishment of the communist regime, for Spain and Barcelona, where he became a legendary player and helped financially support Puskás during his FIFA-imposed ban

Gusztáv Sebes: At once Hungary's Deputy Minister for Sport and the coach of the national team that took over the world in the 1950s. His belief in 'socialist football' and his radical tactical developments underscored the phenomenal talent at his disposal

Señor Ali: AKA Gyula Pollák. Holocaust survivor who lost his wife and daughter in the war; personal secretary to Puskás in Budapest and Madrid; fence for goods smuggled into Hungary by the *Aranycsapat* and alleged informer to the secret police

General Franco: Dictator of Spain from 1939 until his death in 1975 and welcome receiver of defecting footballers from Hungary during the 1950s. Franco allegedly responded to governmental concerns over reprisals from FIFA by asking: "What is FIFA?"

NOBODY'S FOOL

There are misconceptions about the birth of Ferenc Puskás. It has been recorded that he was born in Kispest but he saw the first light of day in a hospital in Józsefváros, another district of Budapest, on April 1, 1927. His birth date is almost always given as April 2, but this was because Puskás did not want it to be known, particularly in the unforgiving atmosphere of the dressing room, that he was born on April Fool's Day. He thus destroyed nearly all the data of his birth date, except that which existed in his passport and was seen by his wife. Thus, he could give the nickname 'Fool' to his verbal sparring partner and Hungarian team-mate Zoltán Czibor, who admitted to being born on April 1.

The Puskás family moved to Kispest, a small town outside Budapest, when the father, Ferenc Purczeld, became a footballer at Kispesti AC at the same time as working at the town hall and was given the chance to rent a flat in one of the tenements near the stadium. Ferenc senior was from a Swabian[1] family from Taksony, just south of Budapest. His grandparents spoke only

---

1   Swabia is a cultural, historic and linguistic region in south-western Germany, taking in the former German state of Württemberg and parts of Bavaria, from which there were waves of migration to Hungary as far back as 1000AD

German; his parents spoke Swabian to each other but Ferenc senior only used Hungarian at home. His wife, Margit, was a farmhand's daughter from Kecskemét. One of young Ferenc's nicknames was 'The Swabian'. 'Öcsi', an affectionate term meaning younger brother, was his nickname at home from a very young age, bestowed upon him by his godmother, and soon this was how he was known all over, even in the Hungarian football press.

Puskás' father had originally trained to be a locksmith but, after moving to Kispest, he mostly earned his living weighing meat at the local abattoir. At one point he was a wine inspector in the local area, but earned his salary as an employee of the town council, a job obtained primarily because he played football for Kispest. He would later nurture his son from the youth teams to the first team, where he became head coach.

In 1937, when his son was 10 years old, he was preparing to take a coaching exam when it was brought to his attention that it would be advantageous to adopt a Hungarian-sounding name. From the two possibilities – Pusztai and Puskás – he chose the latter, which would become the most famous Hungarian word in the world. Just six years later the newspaper *Nemzeti Sport* began referring to him as Ferenc Puskás senior – for Hungarians, the name applied exclusively to his 16-year-old son.

He was baptised in Kispest's Roman Catholic Church where the family attended Mass and where the little Puskás would first take communion and then serve as an altar boy. He never smoked, never even tried it as a boy. This may be because he often had to run errands when his mother had run out of cigarettes. He could not stand tobacco. The other product that Öcsi was regularly forced to buy was Karill, a headache medicine in the form of a suckable sweet. His mother often had a headache, probably because of the hours she spent in the midst of charcoal steam when at work as an ironing lady.

He was an animal-lover and would bring home different creatures, birds or rodents. Once, he found a mouse, put into a fruit jar and made a little ladder for it. The mouse escaped and laid ruin to groceries. Puskás was smacked by an irate mother.

Margit was a cheerful woman until Puskás' exile in 1956. The house was full of love and singing. Öcsi's father had a weakness for *fröccs* – a wine spritzer – and supposedly once drank 34 at one sitting. But his legacy was that on and off the pitch he nurtured one of the best football players in the world.

Sadly, Öcsi wasn't allowed to be at his father's funeral because the national coach wouldn't release him from the team to play a fixture in Poland. It was painful for him, too, that his dad didn't live to see his international successes. He died in 1952, before Hungary won Olympic gold in Helsinki in the same year. Öcsi inherited from him his good heart, his devotion to football and also his favourite song: *Nótás kedvű volt az apám* (*My Father was the Singing Kind*).

Neither could Puskás be at his mother's funeral, as he was in exile by the time she died. When she was alive, his absence was almost unbearable for her, even though after years of separation they were able to meet in Madrid, at the start of the 1960s. She often sang the Hungarian version of the famous Jewish song *My Yiddish Momme*, mainly for its lyric: 'Her jewels and treasures / She found them in her baby's smile.'

Puskás went to two schools in Kispest; for the first four years at a school on Szegfű utca then for another four years at one on Petőfi Sándor utca – or as Öcsi said: "I went there once in a while." That Puskás, in later life, didn't have any problems reading or writing in foreign languages (even in Greek) and that he was a prolific correspondent was probably thanks to his childhood appetite for reading books. If the weather or other circumstances made it impossible for him to play football he would throw himself into bed and read a book, usually a 'cowboys and Indians' novel.

THE CANNONBALL KID

From the kitchen window of his family's small apartment, young Puskás could see the main grandstand of the Kispest stadium – but a fence meant that the 15-year-old had to walk 200 metres to training every day. However, he already had a fan club. Local children built a bridge over the fence from the bricks and other materials left over from the grandstand's renovation, so he could get to training more easily.

There were eight modest, single-storey houses in the street, inside each of which were four flats. These belonged to Kispest town council and were built to accommodate council employees. The flats consisted of one bedroom, a kitchen, a larder or pantry and a small porch; each housed a family, often with four or five children. The bedroom was only kept warm by heat generated in the kitchen and the eight houses were supplied with water from two taps in the courtyard. The toilets were communal.

One summer there were as many as 105 children living in the eight houses and their playground was usually the plot of land behind the houses – the area between the tenements and Kispest's main pitch. The main game was football. There were only two children in the Puskás family, Ferenc and his sister Éva, which was unusually small for the time.

The Puskás' flat was the closest one to the stadium and his first football memory was the roar of the crowd.

During their childhood, Puskás and his friends usually played on two plots of land. One was an area covered with deep, fine sand between the tenements and the stadium and the other was in the grounds of the desolate, uninhabited factory across the street. This had been munitions factory before the First World War. It hosted Puskás, the cannonball kid.

Football was played on these plots of land from dawn until dusk, often with a ball made from rags, because the kids were unable to find a real one, a situation which sometimes lasted for months on end. Éva says that Öcsi's mother's stockings frequently went missing because the prodigy needed them to make these rag-balls. Not only could he destroy the rag-ball by kicking it to pieces with just one swing of his foot, but he was also a master of its preparation. He would create one layer with stuffed rags or grass, after which the stockings were folded on top and the contents squashed up by throwing the ball on to the floor. Then another layer was prepared, and so on, as long as there were still stockings to use or until the ball was the right size. Even so, even the best rag-ball only barely bounced.

The plot of land between the houses consisted of deep sand. It has been said that no modern training system could replicate the environment which imbued the Hungarian players with a superb physical condition. The frightening thighs of Puskás were not created in the gym but on the sand of Kispest.

The surface was also important in order to improve technique because the ball needed to be kicked just a few centimetres above the sand to avoid it changing direction unexpectedly.

A wall separated each house, upon which the millions of ball marks testified to how young Puskás and the other children never grew tired of the ball.

"I don't understand how it was possible to play football so well in such poor footwear as we had," mused Puskás, as he held József Bozsik's old boots in his hands in 1981. However, they were already talented footballers, having played barefoot in their childhood with the rag-ball. It was also possible to buy a rubber football for less than one pengő[2] so sometimes they used one of these, but that was worse than the rag-ball, so the children preferred to save the money.

Occasionally they had the chance to play with a real football, if they could smuggle one away from the club's equipment store, but this was very hard to achieve. Youngsters helped polish the boots of the star players of Kispest, after which they were sometimes allowed to borrow a ball as a reward.

Once, when a young Puskás was unwell, he was left alone at home by his mother who had an errand to do in Budapest. She made him promise not to get out of bed but by the time she arrived home she could not find Öcsi anywhere in the house. Of course, she didn't have to search for him for long because she knew he would be playing football. Furious, she went out to bring him home. But the other children at the plot, seeing her angry demeanour, surrounded him so that he was hardly visible from the ground.

"Please don't hurt him," they implored her. "We need him for the game."

This was the first time that Puskás' footballing ability saved him from trouble. He was five years old.

Öcsi's mother once tore a strip off her young son after he ruined one of his boots. This time his father rose to his son's defence, saying: "The time will come when he won't have to buy boots with his own money because they will be given to him as

---

2   the currency of Hungary between 1927 and 1946. The pengő was subdivided into 100 fillér

a matter of course." What he couldn't have foreseen was that there would be a time when *World Soccer*, the English football magazine, would contain adverts for the latest boots endorsed by his son. Öcsi, after becoming successful in Hungary, received football boots that were specifically made for his feet from the shoemaker of Honvéd – size 41.5, an eight in British terms. Puskás continued to order boots from this shoemaker while he was at Real Madrid and, with one of his friends, tried to initiate the mass production of this special footwear until a large sports-goods firm copied the prototype boots Puskás had given to a small West German team to test out.

ÖCSI AND CUCU

THERE is much of Puskás' story which seems as if it could have been written in a screenplay: his victories with the Magyars over England; the heartache of their defeat in the World Cup final; the incredible tales around some of the escapes from Hungary in the aftermath of the Uprising; his exile and suspension from football; his second, incredible career as a leading player for the great Real Madrid team. Yet the most fantastic element is his relationship with József Bozsik – whose name was always the answer Puskás gave to the question: Who is the greatest player of all time? A question others answered with the word: Puskás.

Honvéd named their stadium after Bozsik. The biggest stadium in Hungary is named after Puskás – the former Népstadion, meaning 'People's Stadium', was originally built to accommodate the many thousands of fans who wanted to see the Magical Magyars. These two players were central to that team's many successes – Puskás scoring the goals, Bozsik running the engine that fuelled the great forward.

After they were separated by the events of 1956 and Puskás starred for Madrid, he was vilified by the communist regime in Hungary. Meanwhile, Bozsik played on for Hungary and Honvéd but lost his roles as a high-ranking officer in the army and a Member of Parliament. But before it all even began, they were neighbours growing up together, their families side-by-side in the same building, playing in the sand and walking to school together.

Bozsik was nicknamed 'Cucu'. Two of his four brothers also played for Kispest's first team and it's generally considered that István, nicknamed 'A Cigány' (the gypsy), was the best player in the family before he died at an early age from pulmonary tuberculosis. According to the cynics, Cucu – who had worked to support his family from a very early age – could just about read and write. Puskás often asked him at autograph signings: "Should I guide your hands?" However, on the pitch he was unanimously regarded as the most intelligent player.

Puskás and Bozsik raced the trams along Sárkány utca, dug holes under fences to get into a big match when ticketless, stole socks to prepare a rag-ball, imitated the moves and told the stories of the footballing aces at Kispest, and carried the bricks and cement for the rebuilding of the Kispest grandstand that burnt down in 1936. The two neighbours even had their own code: a knock on the dividing wall which separated the flats in which they lived meant: Let's play football.

Puskás' first Kispest membership card was made out in the name of Miklós Kovács and also contained a false date of birth.

When Nándi Szűcs, Kispest's handyman and talent scout, sent Öcsi's friend, the 12-year-old Cucu Bozsik, to a photographer saying the club would sign him, Puskás was hurt, asking why he hadn't been approached to sign too. The answer was simple – he was too young. According to the rules you could only be a footballer if you were at least 12 years old. But Öcsi harangued Szűcs – who was fully aware of his beseecher's talent – until he was signed as well.

Puskás and Bozsik clasped their hands together every day

and said: "I believe in one God, I believe in one homeland, I believe in one Godly everlasting truth, I believe in Hungary's resurrection. Amen."[3] This is how it was and, as for any member of that generation, this permeated the inner feelings of patriotism which, for the national football team and its audience, fuelled a huge, unspeakable but common spirit in the fearful years of the 1950s.

The first chances for Kispest's talented players to supplement their basic wage were provided by the club's patrons. Puskás had a short-lived career as a tinsmith, but he also worked in the dangerous and back-breaking business of extracting industrial waste, mostly coke, for tips. 'Cokers' stood in a mine shaft several metres deep and scooped partially burnt pieces of coal upwards to those in charge at the surface. This work was dangerous because the shaft could collapse at any time. Bozsik would stand at the deepest point and he and István Cserjés, his Kispest and then Honvéd team-mate, would shovel the waste up to Puskás. It was possible to sell one sack of coke for good money, but the lads from the tenements usually kept it as their families needed the fuel.

Then there was the ironmongery, shortly after the war. Bozsik and Puskás were given permission to rent the premises with the help of Kispesti AC and for a very short time it looked like they would turn it into a good business. However, the young footballers were not good businessmen. After a few months, the two initially enthusiastic shopkeepers decided to get rid of the shop because they were losing a lot of money.

One of Cucu's brothers, László, recalled: "One day an old lady strayed into our shop but didn't find anyone at the counter

---

3   This is the Hungarian Credo, which was recited in every Hungarian school and at all social events between the two world wars, after Hungary had lost two-thirds of its territory after the First World War.

because Öcsi – who was on duty that day – was hitting the deck [playing cards] with some friends in the storeroom at the back. After a time, the lady shouted in a tired voice that she wanted a large bowl. When there was no answer she called out again, but this time in a firm voice. Puskás shouted back: 'Do not lament, my dear! Get the bowl you want and put the money on the counter.'"

The shop failed, they paid off their debt and then decided to focus on playing football.

They were both wine controllers, too, for a time. They had influence at the town hall not just because both their fathers worked as the employees of the town but also because those at the top of the football club and the town council – who were usually the same people – worked hard to find jobs for the footballers. Wine-controlling was a kind of tax-auditing activity, in which one had to monitor who bought wine from whom and for how much the wine was sold in a bar. Puskás' work at the office was not particularly strenuous.

This was a time of staggering inflation that forced workers to be paid in plates. They could exchange these plates for food.

Ferenc Csutorás was a particularly easy-going individual. He was classified as a kulák[4] at the beginning of the Rákosi[5] regime then was locked up for 'illegal pig-killing' and his house and his land confiscated. Once freed from prison he became a Stakhanovite, a decorated champion worker, who used the change in his situation to ask for the return of his house and his wine bar. These were returned and by the mid '50s he had the business up and running again. He would bring wine produced in Eger to Budapest for sale at, among others, the wine bar

---

4   a prosperous peasant farmer

5   Mátyás Rákosi, leader of the Hungarian Communist party from 1945-56

classified as a 'small co-operative' but to all intent operating as a private business. It was Puskás who helped arrange the permits from the all-powerful authorities for it to open and operate. In exchange, Puskás received 10% of the revenues and the footballers could at any time hold get-togethers, *körözött*[6] -preparing competitions, and wine-drinking with their friends and families in a private room at the establishment which was maintained for them. The bench which the Puskáses took from their villa on Columbus utca to complete the furnishing in the Csutorás wine bar in Eötvös utca today sits in the courtyard of the Csutorás wine cellar in Eger.

Puskás perhaps thought of himself as a successful businessman but the secret service reports don't support this. The operation came to an end after the Uprising and Puskás' departure but continued to work with the help of Károly Sándor[7] for some time after '56. When Csutorás' grandfather refused the compulsory call to join the agricultural co-operative under the Kádár[8] regime, he was once again imprisoned and had to start from scratch. In any case he bequeathed for his son and grandson a beautiful wine cellar, a wonderful trade and the legend of Puskás.

In the latter years of the war and just afterwards, if there was a shortage of food in Budapest then certain footballers were transferred to clubs in the countryside. There was some talk of József Bozsik signing for Kecskemét in exchange for a suit but the buyers changed their minds, later saying: "Cucu's abilities are not worth that much." Ten years later Atlético Madrid offered 100,000 US dollars for his signature.

---

6   spiced sheep cheese with butter

7   Hungarian international team-mate of Puskás

8   János Kádár was leader of the Hungarian Communist Party from 1956 until his retirement in 1988

Puskás' career as a tinsmith was also short lived. His mother spotted him running on the roof – as is normal for a good drain mender – and became so unnerved that she forbade her son to carry on practising the trade. It did not matter for at 16 he was playing in the first division.

After the revolution their roads took very different directions, meaning the old friends only met occasionally in the 'big world' outside Hungary to embrace each other and reminisce. After 1956, Bozsik returned home and continued to play for Honvéd and Hungary for several years, but the earlier successes did not repeat themselves. As a coach he could inspire neither Honvéd nor the national team to their former glories. His only match as manager of Hungary was a 1-0 defeat in Austria in 1974, before he retired due to heart problems. He died in May 1978, a few days before the World Cup in Argentina, where the Hungarian squad wore black armbands in his memory. Puskás, still in exile, was not allowed to attend his funeral in Hungary.

Bozsik's son, Péter, became a footballer and then a manager. He was head coach of Zalaegerszegi TE when they defeated a star-studded Manchester United in the home leg of a UEFA Champions League qualifier in 2002. When, at the press conference before the return match in Manchester, an uninformed journalist asked if his father had ever played on English soil, Bozsik – mindful of the famous 6-3 game when Hungary thrashed England at Wembley in 1953 – pretended to think for a while before answering deadpan: "Well, once for sure…"

Look today for the houses where the two friends grew up and you will not find them, but in a way the old neighbours are as close as ever. On that site now stands the stadium of Honvéd, the Bozsik Stadion. Its address is Puskás Ferenc utca 1-3.

THE RISE OF HONVÉD

PUSKÁS became a Kispest player, but remained a Kispest kid. Even on matchdays, he would be playing football with the children on the estate. His father, by then the head coach of the first team, had to go out and shout at his son: "Finish the game now because you have a first division match this evening."

Even when they were world stars Puskás, Kocsis and the others would play football with the street kids because they simply could not ignore a football if there was one nearby.

Puskás and his friends would also regularly play handball in Kispest and, according to some, Öcsi could have been world-class in this sport, too.

Plaudits were already coming the way of a youthful Öcsi and his team-mates. When Bozsik, Nándor Bányai and other homegrown youngsters made it to the first team, Kispest achieved better and better results. They were a small team before the war, but improved to such a dramatic extent that they finished second in the first division in 1947, fourth in 1948 and third in 1949. If Puskás and the others hadn't done so well, the leaders would hardly have had the idea to establish Kispest as the army's representative sports club. However, because of their recent success and Bozsik and Puskás' prospective leading roles in the national team, the national sports committee changed the balance of power in Hungarian club football so that the spine of the national team could be now gathered together at one club. Thus a surfeit of high-quality footballers congregated at Kispest: goalkeeper Gyula Grosics, central defender Gyula Lóránt, prolific forward Sándor Kocsis and later outside-left Zoltán Czibor. The club name and colours also changed. Kispest became the Hungarian Army team and, in becoming so, created the country's biggest sports club, Budapesti Honvéd. The traditional Kispest fans may have yearned for the former club name and colours but it was a source of great pride that a team mostly consisting of home-grown players won the championship in 1949-50 – before the stars from other clubs arrived. This, their first league title, owed a little to Kispest's history as well. The coach was Ferenc Puskás senior.

In the next few years Budapesti Honvéd developed into possibly the best club team in the world, sweeping all before them on their tours abroad. At the time of the Uprising in 1956 Honvéd were playing lucrative friendly matches throughout Europe, after which they toured Brazil where they were presented with bouquets of flowers and played in sold-out stadiums, but soon this magical team would be no more, broken up by the departure of emigrating stars. Despite this, the name of Honvéd, meaning 'defender of the homeland' and a term of honour dating back to the Hungarian revolt against their Austrian overlords in 1848, remained famous.

UEFA's *Champions* magazine named the coach Béla Guttmann as one of the most successful in football history. His achievements were extraordinary. He built championship-winning teams in Hungary (at Újpest, twice), Italy (AC Milan), Portugal (Benfica and Porto), Holland (Twente Enschede), Uruguay (Peñarol) and Brazil (São Paulo). Furthermore, he won two European Cups with Benfica.

In its summary of Guttmann, the magazine said that "without him the Hungarians may never have beaten England at Wembley; perhaps the successful history of Benfica wouldn't have happened; and in all probability neither would the Brazilian team's 4-2-4 formation exist." This latter strategy was introduced to Brazil using the model of the Magical Magyars.

In 1948 Guttmann, already highly regarded in the football world, became the coach of Kispest, replacing Puskás senior.

The story has been told by lots of people but perhaps the most reliable source is from István 'Pista' Cserjés, who played in the league match in question, in Győr in November 1948. Mihály Patyi of Kispest had been playing in an overly physical manner and the referee had been forced to speak to him more than once. Kispest were already a number of goals behind, the match was all but over and Ferencváros awaited in the next fixture. Guttmann thought it advisable to take off Patyi in order to avoid a possible sending off, so he called from the substitutes' bench for 'Miska' to come off. Immediately Öcsi told the defender: "You stay here!" After a short hesitation, Patyi continued the game. Guttmann's authority had suffered a mortal blow and he reacted by choosing the only professional solution: resignation. At that exact moment he moved from the bench to the grandstand and no one ever saw him with the team again, with Puskás senior resuming control.

That is to say, not until eight years later, when Guttmann joined Honvéd in Vienna, his then residence, just as they began to tour Europe at the time of the Uprising. Guttmann travelled with the touring Honvéd to South America and decided to stay in Brazil, where he found fame and success before returning to Europe to reach the pinnacle of his career in Portugal.

Puskás and Guttmann forgave each other and together they

represented the Hungarian football family around the world. But that is not the end of the story. Their final competitive meeting came in the final of the 1962 European Cup, when Guttmann's Benfica faced Puskás' Real Madrid. The film of the match is a gourmet feast for football lovers. Puskás produced one of the most brilliant performances of his career, but it wasn't enough against Guttman's team which featured the emerging star of European football, Eusébio.

Puskás opened the scoring in Amsterdam's Olympic Stadium when he latched on to Di Stéfano's volleyed pass and ran 50 yards through the middle to fire home. Five minutes later, he doubled *Los Blancos'* lead with a thunderous 30-yard effort. However, Benfica were level within 10 minutes through strikes from Jose Aguas, who knocked in a rebound after Eusébio's free-kick had come back off the post. Cavem then made it 2-2 for the Portuguese, but Puskás restored Madrid's lead before half-time. Guttmann's influence proved key at half-time. Di Stéfano had been dropping deep and dictating play for Madrid with devastating effect so Guttmann assigned Cavem to man-marking duties on the great Argentine. It proved a masterstroke. Mário Coluna equalised and then Eusébio made his mark. The Mozambique-born striker dispatched a 64th-minute penalty after outpacing Di Stéfano and then being fouled in the box, before adding his side's fifth five minutes later. Benfica became European champions for the second year in a row. Puskás, meanwhile, made unwanted history by becoming the only man to score a hat-trick in a European Cup final and still end up on the losing side. After the match, Eusébio sought out Puskás and the two exchanged shirts, beginning a famous friendship that would last for decades.

When asked if he had a mascot, or lucky charm, Puskás said: "No. My mascot was the ball. I only felt safe and secure if the ball was with me." But there were superstitions and eccentricities in Puskás the footballer. The most obvious idiosyncrasy is probably that he played in socks that had a different colour to those of his team-mates. This is against the rules of the game, but after a time there was not a referee at home or abroad who would dare provoke Öcsi.

CAPTAIN OF HUNGARY

IMI MARKOS, the former Swedish correspondent of *Nemzeti Sport*, told me a nice story about Puskás' debut. Imi's father was a well-known footballer and manager in Hungary and Sweden. Once he was waiting for his father in a corridor in the MLSZ[9] headquarters when Tibor Gallowich, a highly-respected coach who never suffered fools gladly, stumbled upon him. He started to talk with little Imi as if he was a peer, at which point he shared with him his chief professional dilemma.

"What do you think? Should I put this kid in? I think I'll put him in."

That kid was Ferenc Puskás. He was introduced into the national team on August 20, 1945, aged 18, and Imi Markos always claimed that, after the manager, he was the first person in Hungary to know of the impending call-up. Puskás scored almost immediately.

In Britain the team captain is an institution within a football team. The player who wears the armband has the greatest authority, leads by example and is often the man most closely associated with the club. In Hungary, the situation is different.

---

9   The Hungarian Football Federation

The captain is usually the best player and has the greatest prestige, but isn't necessarily the club's talisman. Ferenc Puskás was the captain of the team in every sense.

In the national team he wasn't the oldest by any means – there was Nándor Hidegkuti who was five years older and universally respected; there was József Bozsik and the fearless professional Gyula Lóránt. Even then, the captain of the team was Öcsi.

He wasn't elected by his team-mates, but everyone accepted him. Öcsi became the captain of the team because he was the best of the many talents there. However, he happened to be well-suited to this special position on and off the pitch. On the pitch he became almost like a player-coach, a role which came naturally to him, and if it was necessary he would change tactics during matches. He could assess in seconds where the opposition's strengths and weaknesses lay and issued instructions accordingly, in his own inimitable style. For example, the early part of a match against Italy in Rome in 1953 was notable only for a series of dangerous headers from the host's striker, Galli. After the latest effort, Öcsi said to Lóránt fiercely: "Lóri! How long is this kid going to be doing that?"

The centre-half understood he had to address the situation and the next time he contested a header with Galli, kicked the poor Italian so hard in the midriff that the forward had to be taken from the pitch.

Puskás was the captain of the team even when the national team was not together. Jenő Buzánszky, the right-back for that Hungary side, remembers Puskás looking after him even when their clubs faced each other.

Honvéd played a league match in Dorog, a town between Budapest and the Slovak border, and Buzánszky (the only member of the *Aranycsapat* who did not play football for the two big Budapest teams of the time; Honvéd and MTK) was in pain with a troublesome injury. Despite this, he desperately wanted to play against Honvéd and swathed his leg in bandages to dull the pain of the kicks he would receive. Puskás noticed this and scolded him, asking why he wanted to jeopardise his place in the national team match the following week. Buzánszky refused to budge from his decision and lined up for the game. Puskás, seeing this, called in his Honvéd team-mates and told them forcefully: "Anyone who hurts Jenő today will get a kick in the arse from me!" Buzánszky adds at the end of the story that "we beat Honvéd 1-0".

"I hadn't expressed a desire to take the captaincy but sometime around 1949 I was appointed captain of Hungary. I feel like I'm still that even today."

Ferenc Puskás said this after his homecoming in 1981. His team-mates would always meet in the Régi Sipos restaurant and I saw how they saluted him when they arrived and left, sometimes even calling him 'captain'. Puskás would sit at the head of the table, put his two fingers into his mouth and give a loud whistle at the sound of which, all the players would instantly stop the chatter and turn their heads towards him. Even in his older years, he had a frightening authority over the team.

Puskás had a hand in Lóránt playing in the axis of the defences of both Honvéd and the national team. Puskás was said to dislike playing against Lóránt. The defender, who hailed from Nagyvárad and moved from the local professional club to Vasas in Budapest, was one of the chief organisers of a famous attempt to defect from Hungary in 1949, only for the plot to be uncovered. Even worse for him, as one of the ringleaders Lóránt was arrested and imprisoned in an internment camp in Kistarcsa. The one-time Benedictine student of Kőszeg, a town in western Hungary close to the Austrian border, was now in a very difficult situation. Puskás intervened, and Lóránt was released and allowed to restart his career. Many saw Lóránt as the one who would look out for Öcsi on the pitch in the national team and later at Honvéd as well, when the tough defender was transferred there. Puskás and Lóránt roomed together when on tour or at training camps, at least in the national team.

It was the task of Lóránt to mix and cool his room-mate's drink of choice, *fröccs*.

Mischievous behaviour was always one of Puskás' main characteristics. According to a tale from the 100th Hungary-Austria match in 1955, Puskás and Czibor had a bet at the expense of Imre Schlosser, the bow-legged and elderly Hungarian football legend who was about to perform the ceremonial kickoff. It balanced on how many times Czibor could crawl through between the old man's legs in the centre circle without him noticing.

Puskás liked a wager. There would be small bets on who would win a foot-tennis match or how many times they could hit the crossbar with the ball from the edge of the penalty area. The stake would normally be a *pacalpörkölt* (tripe stew) or a few *fröccs*. There was also the Hungarian card game *ulti* which until recently remained the main entertainment of the country's footballers.

Puskás was a key member of the card parties, alongside Kocsis, Czibor, and Sándor. According to Zoltán Czibor, 'Csikar' Sándor, who didn't make the official squad for the World Cup in Switzerland, was brought along with the delegation so he could be the fourth man in the card games.

He was a card sharp before then, however. László Bozsik and István Cserjés mentioned this passion as being a major component of the young Puskás' life. As a teenager he would play *huszonegy* (a variant of blackjack with Hungarian cards) and *ferbli*, another game, with his friends for hours on end. On hot summer nights they would often go out to the empty football ground at Kispest and lay the cards out on the seats of the stands, playing for a few coins until such time as a passing policeman would send them home.

He had an interest in medicine. Later, during the long training camps, he would often question László Kreisz, the national team doctor, or Tamás Fried, Honvéd's doctor, about the treatment of injuries and ailments. Puskás not only treated his own injuries successfully but also gave advice to family members.

Fried, who lived in Canada in his later years, wrote in his memoirs that in his professional opinion the Germans were using drugs at the World Cup in Berne in 1954, where they defeated Hungary in the final.

PUSKÁS' WAR

"NEITHER father nor Öcsi were ever soldiers, thank God!" said Éva Puskás, his sister. However, she is very much mistaken, since Öcsi wasn't just a soldier; as the world came to know, he was a major. The 'Galloping Major' nickname is known worldwide. He was an officer who never held a weapon. Puskás' most brutal piece of action came on the pitch in Bulgaria, when he struck a defender in retaliation, and then in Greece when he reputedly kicked one of the AEK Athens bosses firmly between the legs before handing in his notice. In Rotterdam, after a European Cup tie in 1965, he kicked a fan who had invaded the pitch. This was the closest he came to combat.

The Puskás family survived the Second World War because they always had enough food. Öcsi's father worked at the abattoir, so they could barter meat for products such as cottage cheese and sour cream at a time when some in Budapest were forced to shoot their horses for food.

They briefly moved to the countryside region of Pilis, where the town council rented rooms for its employees. During the weeks of the Siege of Budapest[10] abattoir workers and their

---

10   the 50-day long encirclement of Budapest by Soviet forces near the end of the Second World War

families hid themselves in the air-raid shelter of the abattoir in Kispest. Öcsi Puskás, still just a youth, spent some time in Pilis but generally stayed in the air-raid shelter during these months, waiting for the end of the war.

Puskás turned 18 in the bloodiest year of the War for Hungary. Zoltán Czibor, his team-mate, and two years his junior, was conscripted and Puskás may be considered fortunate not to have shared his fate. It is said that it was because of football that he didn't become a soldier.

He made his debut in the Hungarian first division at the end of 1943 and by the following year his name was already known nationwide. Many footballers could thank their fame for avoiding the front. A memorable example was the Ferencváros winger László Gyetvai who at the last minute was 'plucked' from a train about to leave for the Eastern front due to the intervention of his legendary team-mate György Sárosi. There were also those who carried out their duties in the capital so that they could play football at the same time.

However, Öcsi once came very close to being made a soldier on the front. It happened in 1944 after the Nyilas[11], came to power. After a few drinks Bozsik and Puskás were walking home late at night when they came across two Nyilas members standing around the neighbouring tenement blocks. One of them, a Mr Cziegel, who had been a neighbour of the boys, asked them what they were doing there when their country was bleeding and told them that they should be in the firing line. The two boys didn't know what to say. They were taken to the nearby headquarters where other freshly enlisted comrades in misfortune waited.

At this time every man above the age of 16 faced compulsory

---

11   Hungarian fascist movement – the Arrow Cross

military service. The 17-year-old Puskás and the 19-year-old Cucu Bozsik seemed ideal cannon fodder. Their only bit of luck was that Károly Monostori, who held a higher rank than Cziegel, was present, and who – through being a former Kispest player himself – knew the latest pair of arrivals. He was a first-rate footballer and a sensitive man who saved the two boys from the army and perhaps even from death. He snapped at them: "Well, what are you doing here? Go home!"

From then on they didn't go out at night and laid low until the end of the war, practically as runaways from the army (Bozsik even went to the countryside), successfully avoiding the draft.

Kispest trained and played while it was still possible. Éva Puskás remembers that when the family moved to Pilis during the bombing and the fiercest battles in Budapest her father and elder brother still went in to Kispest for training. League matches were still played even in the spring of 1944. The Hungarian international Ferenc Rudas, for example, went to play the Ferencváros–Kispest match on March 19, 1944 – the exact date of the Nazi invasion of Hungary – after soldiers' drill. Someone told him to watch out because "Kispest have a talented 16-year-old kid".

Rudas, as a national team big-shot, paid scant regard to the warning. However, as he recalled: "We hadn't even shouted 'Hurrah! Hurrah!' [a Hungarian custom] prior to kick-off before he'd already slipped in twice beside me and scored two goals."

In February 1945 the fighting came to an end in Kispest and Bozsik and Puskás soon played football with the more friendly of the Soviet soldiers. Kispest were playing again by the end of April 1945 after an 11-month hiatus. Four months later, on August 20, St Stephen's Day, the second of two international friendly matches on consecutive days was held between Hungary and Austria. This game would provide a double celebration for

Puskás: his first appearance and first goal for the national team. It was also the first game covered by György Szepesi, a radio commentator who would become the chief chronicler of the story of the *Aranycsapat* for the Hungarian people.

After the war Kispest improved and politicians attached more importance to sport. Moscow gave the order that sports associations of the armed forces and large trade unions had to be brought into existence in all socialist countries. This happened in Hungary at the end of 1949.

Had it not been for the emergence of Kispest, powered by Puskás and Bozsik, it is certain they and others would have been redeployed into the Ferencváros team which was already packed with national team stars. Instead, the best young players were ordered to join them at Honvéd, and represent the army.

The world was turned upside down for the Kispest footballers. They became the favourites of the regime. The club announced it was changing its name to Budapesti Honvéd and was joining the People's Army. Honvéd became in Budapest what CSKA had in Moscow and Sofia, Dukla in Czechoslovakia, Partizan in Belgrade, and Legia in Warsaw.

After changes to the club name and colours came the forced signings, dictated from above. It is quite true that the gathering of star players at one club was for the benefit of the national team, but it ridiculed club loyalty and showed contempt towards the supporters.

For Sándor Kocsis, László Budai (both Ferencváros) or Gyula Grosics (Teherfuvar) it was a great opportunity to sign for Honvéd, the elite team, but for Kocsis it also posed an unusual moral dilemma. The family had been Ferencváros fans for generations but the press didn't explain to the supporters that the footballers had been given an ultimatum: "Join Honvéd and light duties await you in Budapest, or you'll be taken to be a border guard for three years somewhere far away in the countryside." In the absence of correct information, many old *Fradistas*[12] couldn't forgive the players for transferring.

The great goal king Ferenc Deák, for example, was forced with even uglier blackmail from Ferencváros to Újpest. He was arrested for beating up two ÁVH (secret police) men who told him to sign for Újpesti Dózsa or he would rot in jail.

Budapesti Honvéd became the best football team in the world. The majority of the national team players sooner or later ended up beside Puskás and Bozsik. These included Grosics, Lóránt, Budai, Kocsis and Czibor, complemented with, among others, László Rákóczi, Nándor Bányai and later Lajos Tichy and Ferenc Machos. Those national team players who didn't end up at Honvéd played for the state security team, formerly named MTK, operating under the different guises of Textiles, Bástya and Vörös Lobogó. Here were Nándor Hidegkuti, Péter Palotás, Károly Sándor, József Zakariás, Mihály Lantos, Sándor Gellér, János Börzsey and Imre Kovács. From the countryside, only Jenő Buzánszky (at Dorog) and Ferenc Szojka (at Salgótarján) were permanent national squad members.

"It was the most amusing period of Öcsi's life," said his wife on hearing the words Sport Squadron. The communists tried to chisel soldiers out of the Budapesti Honvéd sportsmen. They were conscripted amidst much fanfare before beginning training. They lived for three months in barracks but, after many pranks, the superiors felt it better if the sportsmen continued their official careers at home.

Apart from Puskás, the other main character in the Sports Squadron was a legendary prankster, the boxer Lajos Fehér,

---

12 Ferencváros fans

whom everyone knew as Pacal (Tripe) after his favourite food. One day Pacal Fehér went to Puskás on behalf of the wrestlers and boxers: "Öcsi! We'd like to invite you to play a five-a-side football match."

"What the blazes? Within two minutes you'll be ten down and you'll run to your mothers saying that we are mistreating you," replied Puskás.

"Not at all," said Pacal Fehér innocently. "We only want to say to our grandchildren that we played against you."

Puskás smelled a rat. "Don't give me that bull, don't mess me around! This had better not be a trick."

"Of course not."

"Ok, when?"

"Tomorrow, but everyone should wear heavy boots!"

"That's stupid, should we wear fur-caps too?"

The following day one of the teams lined up: Szilvásy, Növényi, Záhorszky, Molnár, Simon – all of them strapping fellows.

Against them were the football stars: Grosics, Bozsik, Kocsis, Czibor and Puskás. Everyone in heavy boots.

Öcsi and the others could hardly manage to lift their feet off the ground and they were muscled off the ball whenever they had it. Physical strength overcame great technique and after the two 30-minute halves, four footballers were taken to the sick-bay and the team couldn't take the field for the training match scheduled for later that day. Puskás said in the changing room: "I'm glad I'm still in one piece. I'll recommend them to the army as tanks."

Someone in the Sport Squadron had to be on duty every day and report to the Defence Ministry on whether anything had happened. Once Puskás was the officer on duty, and his deputy was Pacal Fehér. Öcsi was already bored of the whole thing but still couldn't break the rules. When the time came, Pacal went to him.

"Öcsi, it's 10pm. Report to the Ministry."

"I'm knackered," Puskás replied. "Report in for me, but don't overdo it."

Pacal went over to the telephone and dialled the number of the directorate.

"Hello, Ferenc Puskás speaking! 6-3, 7-1, Olympic gold. Everything's cool in the Sport Squadron, no trouble! By the way, you should promote Pacal Fehér tomorrow."

The writer Ferenc Karinthy once said that an anecdote doesn't always have to be true. Presumably this is the case with this tale, taken from the 1981 book *Puskás – Legenda és valóság (Legend and Reality)*. The three months spent in the Sport Squadron preceded the 6-3 game by years.

"They were worldly, that's for sure!" laughed Erzsébet when I asked about this 'playing at soldiers'.

"Did they wear uniform? Oh yes. But the socks were all different colours and they wore street shoes.

"I know there was a tiny wrestler, Páger. They made a lot of pranks together. Ask Gyula Grosics, apparently they hung him out of the window."

Puskás, still chuckling with laughter even decades afterwards, recalled that at marching practice he talked with the huge basketball players at the head of the line and told them they had to take the biggest steps they could. The average-sized footballers struggled to keep the tempo, while at the end of the line were the flyweight wrestlers at the back taking huge leaps and unable to keep step with the rest.

The Honvéd player István Cserjés, called up at the end of 1949, also remembered Pacal Fehér's pranks, claiming Pacal was unable to hit anywhere near the target during shooting practice and also that there was once an occasion when he was within an ace of a grenade exploding in his hand. Cserjés though, doesn't view these romanticised times in the Sport Squadron through the same rose-tinted spectacles.

"It's not true that Öcsi and the others didn't have to shoot, and the like. Everyone certainly went through the same training. A bit easier of course and with a bit less discipline than the other soldiers, but we went to drill and shooting practice just like everyone else. Öcsi and the others, too."

It is perhaps a little tenuous to mention the *Aranycsapat's* last Moscow match in connection with military tactics but it is by no means impossible to do so. It was a historic and bizarre moment. The Magical Magyars took to the field at the inauguration of the 100,000 capacity Lenin Stadium in Moscow a month to the day before the Hungarian Uprising in October 1956. This is the team that had never been able to triumph over the Soviets away from home until that day. Zoltán Czibor got the goal, and afterwards returned to the dressing-room corridor with the provocative shout: "We've beaten communism."

"He received a uniform. It's true that he never wore it but I know that he was proud of it," said Erzsébet. After the change of political system in Hungary, her husband was also rehabilitated as a soldier.

He became a retired officer of the Hungarian army. He returned to his former club, which even then was still sponsored by the army. The club returned to its old colours of red and black and also partially to its former name when it became Kispest Honvéd (for some reason it is now called Budapest Honvéd again) and as a sensible compromise, seemed to respect both previous pasts.

After his return from exile in 1981, Puskás was a permanent visitor to the team's matches for as long as his health would permit. He would still make jokes and give advice to the coaches and players who respected and adored him. He became a member of the club's management, took part in many celebrations, drank wine spritzers and played cards in the clubhouse.

The celebrity and importance of Puskás as a national hero gave him the power to influence, to change and to save lives. Early one morning in 1955, Zoltán Czibor, the brilliant outside-left, dressed in his army uniform, ordered the waiters of the EMKE restaurant to perform a series of exercises and drills on the streets. Unbeknown to him, the waiters were also informers of the Hungarian secret police. Puskás saved him from impeachment.

It was a frightful story – we can't grasp how real the threat of capital punishment was for such crimes – but it was typically black and white for Puskás: "Will you play at outside-left on Sunday?" he asked Mihály Farkas, the Minister of National Defence.

This was a ploy he had used previously to save other errant players. However, he knew Czibor's wellbeing was at stake this time, so he brought with him his close friend and team-mate József Bozsik, the regime's poster boy.

The influence of Puskás allowed György Kárpáti, three-time Olympic water polo champion, to be admitted to study law despite having scored zero points in the official entrance examination. Öcsi went to see Farkas and told him: "You ramble on about studying all the time and now here's a man who is very stupid, yet he wants to study. Why don't you let him?"

The result: Karpati was invited by telegram to meet with the university rector so he could be personally informed that he had gained admission to the faculty of law.

The only matter that we know of in which Puskás failed

was the case of Sándor Szűcs. Szűcs was a central defender for Újpest and won 19 caps for the Hungarian national side between 1941 and 1948. Later, he lost his place in the team and perhaps he left for the West because he knew there was no chance of international success in Hungary. However, he and his fiancee, the singer Erzsi Kovács, were caught at the border. He was arrested and condemned to death.

Puskás went to Farkas to plead for the player's life. By the time he could speak to the Minister, his former team-mate had been hanged.

Ferenc Puskás, the dissident footballer of Budapest Honvéd and a deserting officer, was sentenced to death by the relevant Hungarian authorities when he decided to defect. It was only 25 years after committing his crime, in 1981, that he could step on Hungarian soil once more. However, by that time the propaganda aimed at ensuring Puskás be forgotten had already met with much success. Many in the 1980s thought that he was dead. A member of a state folk group once recognised Puskás at Paris airport but was told: "Get a grip! Puskás died ages ago."

Following Puskás' death I was given access to the three, single-page documents which ended any dubiety over whether or not a criminal proceeding had been initiated against him.

The Military Attorney case was initiated under number B. II.2940/1957 pertaining to "the crime of absconding abroad together with other soldiers" on the basis of the Hungarian Criminal Code 313. para. (2), point c.

I looked up the law, for which punishment is ascribed to be "from 10 to 15 years' imprisonment or death".

They could even have carried out such a sentence abroad, with the help of the secret services, as they had done before. From the file on Puskás we know why this course of action was not pursued – they didn't want to make him a martyr. If they had, they would have harmed themselves. Rather, they attempted to keep him in checkmate for decades and deter others from absconding. And their plan worked.

THE MAGICAL MAGYARS

The strain was considerable on the Hungarian side that entered the Olympic Games of 1952 in Helsinki. The preparation had been rigorous. The Stalinist regime in Budapest wanted nothing other than a victory from the Golden Squad.

Gusztáv Sebes, the national coach, had the advantage of having most of his players in one side, Honvéd. He also played midweek matches against smaller clubs to test both strategy and selection.

Hungary arrived in Helsinki confident of victory. They defeated Romania 2-1, then Italy 3-0, Turkey 7-1 in the quarters and the reigning champions Sweden 6-0 in the semi-final.

Warlike hysteria surrounded the Olympic final. The match against Yugoslavia fell in a period when there was no greater enemy in the Soviet sphere of influence than the 'imperialist agent' Tito, who had split from Stalin, and the non-aligned, socialist Yugoslavia under his leadership. In Hungary, the press was also awash with denunciation of the Titoists and demands for their punishment. Tito received the name the 'chained dog of the imperialists' as a permanent epithet.

Before the outstanding Yugoslavia team met Hungary in the final, they first played against the Soviet Union. After the dramatic first match was drawn, the Soviets lost the return and Stalin reputedly became so furious that he banished the whole Soviet Olympic team to the Gulag. In this atmosphere, the Hungarian team prepared for the game against the 'chained dogs', although there may have been reward, as well as risk for the footballers. Gyula Lóránt claimed he was promised a sports car if they won.

The agitation among the communist leadership inspired some typically totalitarian contingency plans. In the event of a Yugoslav victory the Hungarian radio broadcast was to be discontinued and passed off as a technical problem.

Mátyás Rákosi, leader of the Communist Party in Hungary and the de facto ruler of the country, reputedly called the team and Sebes in Helsinki during half-time in the final when the match stood at 0-0 and a missed Puskás penalty had frayed their nerves. In the second half, Puskás was set up by Czibor and then returned the favour. Hungary won 2-0 and Öcsi received the Olympic gold medal from the Finnish Miss World.

It is impossible to appreciate fully the import of the drubbings inflicted on England by the *Aranycsapat*. An aggregate score of 13-4 points to the severity of the defeats at Wembley on November 25, 1953, and in Budapest on May 23, 1954. But it does not even hint at the significance of the results, particularly at Wembley.

There was, at that time, an acceptance that England were invincible on their own turf. No team outside Great Britain and Ireland had proved this theory wrong. England turned up at Wembley and trounced the 'fancy dans' of Europe and beyond with their continental pretensions to possession football that evaporated on contact with the ruthless home side.

It was dubbed 'The Match of the Century'. A distinctly

unoriginal title did contain an element of truth. The Hungarians changed forever the way football was played. They dealt a fatal blow to the supremacy of the English game at its very root.

Undefeated since 1950, the Hungarians employed Nándor Hidegkuti in a withdrawn role behind Puskás and Sándor Kocsis. England could not handle the tactics, were outdone by pace and technique and were almost relieved to lose 6-3.

Tom Finney, one of the greatest players of that age and any other era, was succinct in his assessment of Hungary. He told Rogan Taylor in *Puskás on Puskás*: "They were the greatest national side I played against. It was like cart horses playing racehorses."

Hungary had a cadre of players who could audition for roles in any all-time XI. There was László Budai, József Bozsik, Kocsis, Hidegkuti, Zoltán Czibor and, of course, Puskás who scored a goal of such technique and venom that it is remembered more than 60 years on. The forward, facing a lunging challenge by Billy Wright, drew the ball back and despatched it immediately into the net with his left foot.

The Hungarians were fit, fast but also brutally and beautifully efficient. A mark of their class was that the England side, previously unbeaten by foreign forces, contained Gil Merrick, Alf Ramsey, Wright, Stanley Matthews and Stan Mortensen.

The return match in Budapest made the Wembley rout seem a closely fought affair. Puskás scored two in a match where England had restored Finney. He could only admire the play that swirled around him.

It was now obvious that a new way of playing football had been refined and it was both entertaining and devastating. The tactics of Sebes had been slightly adjusted but basically the English defence were confounded again by Hidegkuti reprising his deep-lying centre-forward role and the inter-changing between all the forwards. The Hungarians were also too quick for England.

"Six or seven of them deserve to be ranked among the best the world has ever seen," said Finney.

The English side trudged from the Népstadion demoralised and routed. Hungary marched on to Switzerland for a World Cup that surely now lay within their grasp. They had been unbeaten for four years. They had won Olympic gold and now they had thrashed the one-time rulers of the game. What could go wrong?

Puskás was in great form during the team's preparations for the World Cup, and in the 9-0 thrashing of South Korea in the first group match, in which he scored twice. In the following group game against West Germany he was kicked from pillar to post, with the defender Werner Liebrich his principal assailant. As Puskás headed off the pitch at half-time he told Jupp Posipal, the West German player who also spoke Hungarian, to tell "that clumsy oaf to stop" or he would dedicate the rest of the match to humiliating his opponent at every opportunity. However, it was Liebrich who won the duel, when yet another heavy tackle damaged Puskás' ankle – an injury that would keep him out of both the quarter and the semi-final of the tournament.

Hungary won the match 8-3, but West Germany, it turned out, were playing the long game. Having defeated Turkey in their first match, Sepp Herberger, their manager, knew they could lose to Hungary and still qualify if they won a play-off against the Turks. For the group match against Hungary he made seven changes, swallowed the loss and refreshed his team for an easy win in the play-off. Liebrich also ensured the impact of the group game on Hungary was not so easy to overcome.

Without Puskás, Hungary won through two gruelling knockout matches against Brazil – when Bozsik was sent off, along with two Brazilians – and Uruguay – to meet West Germany again in the final.

As Puskás fought to regain his fitness in time for the World Cup final, thousands of telegrams arrived at the national team's accommodation wishing him an early recovery, a chiropractor presented himself at the hotel offering his expertise and even the West German national team's medical personnel offered their help to the Hungarian doctor.

Puskás, restored to the side despite his ankle injury, and Czibor put the Hungarians two up within 10 minutes. But the West Germans fought back to win 3-2, with the winning goal coming with just six minutes to play.

In the aftermath of a historic defeat, there were claims that the Germans had used amphetamine-type drugs; that Puskás, half-fit, took the field only so, as captain, it would be he who lifted the Jules Rimet trophy.

The day after the final, an announcement at Debrecen train station claimed the World Cup final would be replayed as the linesman's flag which had denied Puskás an equalising goal had been proven unjust. People danced and fell into each other's arms, but not for long.

The aftermath was cruel to the one-time heroes. "Everyone was looking for someone to blame," said Puskás, who bore much of the brunt of the disaffection toward a team who had merely won Olympic gold, twice humiliated one of the sport's super-powers and finished runners-up in the World Cup.

THE MATCH OF THE CENTURY

HUNGARY'S 6-3 win over England at Wembley is one of football's landmark results. The game stands as a pivotal moment in the history of the sport. It is world famous – except, for the longest time, in Hungary.

Television wasn't available in Hungary in 1953 but the BBC recorded the whole match. It was broadcast in cinemas, on television and eventually made available as a video recording. Just not in Hungary.

There, it was treated as some kind of state secret. After the exile of Puskás and his team-mates, the story of the *Aranycsapat* was not one the regime was interested in telling. Those who had not returned after the events of 1956 were not heroes and were not to be celebrated.

Football disappeared from Hungary. After all, the game had been deprived of its two essential motivating forces: the money produced by it and the role models which inspired the system.

There was the occasional private home screening covertly arranged using film archives by those privileged enough to access them. For example, Gusztáv Sebes, the former national team coach, had films of old matches. He often screened the 6-3 game at his home, complete with snacks for children who played on the local playground. One of these children was Tibor Nyilasi, who would play more than 70 times for Hungary. Apart from these rare, underground screenings of the goals, no-one could see even a minute of action from the fixture known since then as 'The Match of the Century'.

So it was that at Christmas time in 1996, half the country sat down for a television special showing the whole 90 minutes for the first time on Hungarian television. In the opening credits there was a message which stated the film was the British Embassy's present to Hungary on the occasion of the 1100th anniversary of the Magyar tribes' settlement in the country.

Before Christmas of 2008, Hungarians could for the first time buy a DVD of the most famous match in the history of their national football team. Two more years passed before the DVD of Puskás' other world-famous match, the 1960 European Cup final, was premiered in the Corvin cinema, Budapest, with the first Hungarian commentary being provided after 50 years by the 88-year-old György Szepesi. Both this and the original English commentary were available when the match was shown in the Uránia cinema as a part of the city of Pécs' European Capital of Culture programme.

On the day of the 7-1 game (the *Aranycsapat*'s second victory over England, this time in Budapest in 1954) a family friend of *Aranycsapat* member József Zachariás was on the way home from Pécs to Budapest. He was in a hurry and was travelling on his motorbike through villages as the match unfolded. Everyone was sitting in the streets, huddled around radios, listening to the match together and as he made for Budapest the score would be updated for him from one village to the next. Jubilant people signalled to him with their fingers how many goals Puskás and the others had scored.

The friend was philosophical. He had already exchanged his

two match tickets for a telephone connection, which at that time was more precious than gold.

It is rare that a book is written and a film made about a single football match, but this happened more than once in Puskás' career. First, there was the 6-3 match. László Feleki, who reported for the Hungarian newspaper *Népsport* from London, wrote a splendid book with the same title about the match and its background. A feature film, also called '6-3', was shot in Hungary in 1998. Soon after the matches, *Népsport* published two booklets: one entitled '6-3', the other '7-1', to celebrate these two world-famous victories.

Many years later, the 50th anniversary saw : Péter Török and Sándor Margay publish a beautiful book entitled '6-3 – The Match of the Century'.

Readers sent hundreds of poems to the editorial desk of *Népsport* after the first win against England. Of course, hardly any of these poems have survived the 54 years since the game but Zoltán Zelk's 6-3 poem – 'The Rhyming Greeting Telegram' – is one that has.

The 6-3 match was not the only one of Puskás' to have been commemorated to such an extent. The World Cup final followed a year later, about which a documentary film, *Das Wunder von Bern – The Miracle of Berne* – was released in Germany on the game's 50th anniversary in 2004. The World Cup final also inspired the eminent Hungarian poet Lőrinc Szabó to begin writing.

There is a book in German also entitled 'The Match of the Century', but this isn't about the 6-3 match, nor the final in Bern. However, Puskás plays the lead role in this story, as well. This time it is the European Cup final in Glasgow in 1960 which earns that accolade, despite a heavy 7-3 loss for Eintracht Frankfurt.

The Wembley victory and the 1960 European Cup final – two of the most famous games in the history of football – share one trait: after both victories there were a million people waiting to pay homage to the winners. Following the 6-3 match, people in Budapest waited for the Hungarian national team from Keleti train station all the way down to the River Danube a mile away and, after the 7-3 victory, fans of Real Madrid waited for the team in the downtown area of the Spanish capital. In both cities, Puskás was the most celebrated of the returning heroes.

A lifetime later, Puskás learned of a close relative of one of the players he managed for Panathinaikos, who was in need of life-saving heart surgery. Puskás suggested that he travel to England and there seek the advice of his old adversary Billy Wright, whose tackle he had so brilliantly avoided in scoring the goal that gave the 6-3 game its signature moment.

For the journey, just a couple of notes were given to be handed to Wright. The Greek patient received everything he needed and Wright said: "If Ferenc sent you, it is as if my own brother would have sent you."

PUSKÁS THE SMUGGLER

Even at the height of the international fame enjoyed by the players of Honvéd and Hungary, the regime would not raise their meagre earnings. In this socialist ethos, the athlete was strictly amateur. However, the same athlete was provided a sham job, which he or she hardly ever attended, yet from which they drew their wage. On top of that was a small sum known as 'calorie money' and, in the case of the footballers, a small bonus for winning the league championship. In the 1950s a national team player could earn 4000 forints[13] without smuggling. This was three times the national average, but ridiculously low when compared to the earnings of footballers in Austria, Italy or the other countries now visited by Puskás and his team-mates.

To bridge the chasm between this income and the Western market value of their talents, the athletes were part of a smuggling enterprise condoned – encouraged, even – by the state.

Puskás once referred to the match against Switzerland, when Hungary turned around a 2-0 deficit to win 4-2, as 'the watchmakers against the watch smugglers'.

The players who left after the turmoil of the 1956 revolution

---

13   The currency of Hungary

had hordes of smuggled goods hidden in their Hungarian homes. At their staging post in Italy in December 1956 there was a queue at the only telephone while players briefed their families on the various hiding places such as chimneys and ovens ("Don't light it up, the stove is full of stuff," Czibor warned).

When one player's mother-in-law joyfully told how she'd exchanged her flat for a larger one in the same building, the player exploded: "Have you gone mad? Move back straight away!" Hundreds of gold watches were bricked up in the walls of the old apartment.

The process of smuggling was refined. It became more efficient and grew from bringing in a few pairs of nylon stockings or a gold watch. It went something like this: the goods would be waiting for the teams in Vienna. They didn't need to search for goods and package them themselves. Instead, they had agents abroad who seem to have had a friendly and close connection with the Hungarian secret intelligence agency. These agents bought the goods and sold them to the athletes for foreign currency.

Although the players joked a lot about it, they had some real difficulties when it came to smuggling the goods into Hungary because they all bore personal responsibility. If the team won, it was easy, but if they lost, they became a lot more nervous and the customs inspectors were given signed footballs and other mementos to grease the wheels.

Once back in Hungary there were people who would take the goods in bulk and sell them on nationwide. Everyone involved had their share of profit in this business and all the while the state didn't have to pay a penny more in wages to the athlete-smugglers.

The whole operation also provided useful leverage for the

regime, which held the threat of arrest over the footballers. At the same time, state officials could also fend off requests for increased wages from the athletes. Mihály Farkas, the Minister of National Defence, told Puskás on such an occasion: "Just carry on smuggling because we can't pay you anything."

Everyone was balanced on a tightrope and after the World Cup final loss in 1954 some started to fall. The police caught some of the team in the act of smuggling – whoever they wanted. For example, Grosics and the reserve goalkeeper sent a busload of goods from Vienna which was intercepted at the border. This was the first time this had happened and a sure sign that the footballers were in danger. Terrifyingly, Grosics was arrested and held at the secret police headquarters for days before being released under house arrest. He was subsequently banned from the national team for 18 months and banished to play for countryside club Tatabánya. The treatment inhibited him for the rest of his life.

Another player was stopped at customs and asked what was in a box he was bringing in.

"Bird seed," he replied.

The Hungarian border guard pointed out on opening the box that it contained premium coffee.

The player replied: "Whether it eats it or not, it won't get anything else."

THE GATHERING STORM

IN THE period immediately following the war, and before the communist takeover of power in 1948-49, Puskás and his Hungary team-mates were frequently approached by foreign clubs. In this brief window, however, there was a professionalism in Hungarian football which would soon be gone, and it was harder to prise the jewels of the *Aranycsapat* away. Puskás, for example, could buy a house from the money he received from his guest appearance in Mexico as a Ferencváros player, as well as the amount he got for signing his contract with Kispest. Ferenc Deák, another great forward, owned lodging houses until these buildings were nationalised after the revolution. This professionalism also made it possible for those who saw better opportunities abroad to leave Hungary without any particular trouble. This is how László Kubala went from Ferencváros to Slovan Bratislava in 1946, or Dr. György Sárosi and István Mike went to Italy. However, by the time Kubala had slipped away again in 1949 (after his return home to Vasas) the sports newspaper *Népsport* demanded a life-long ban and depicted him in a caricature as a future alcoholic and homeless person, wandering the streets of Italy. That's not how things worked out for him. Instead, he became one of the greatest players in the history of Barcelona and today his statue can be found in the grounds of the Camp Nou.

Once the communist regime was in place, it was not so easy to get out. A famous attempt to defect was at least in part led by Gyula Lóránt in 1948, but the big stars of the time were also in on it. According to their plans, they would have formed an unbeatable team together in Italy under the name of *Hungária*. Puskás wasn't involved in this but a good few Ferencváros players were, as was the *Aranycsapat* goalkeeper Gyula Grosics. He was the only one to go to the designated leaving point – the others already knew that the plot had been uncovered and so had aborted the plan. This was the first time that Grosics was a 'guest' of the secret police. Lóránt and two Ferencváros players, József Mészáros and Károly Kéri, were arrested and locked up in the Kistarcsa detention camp, the latter two being released with difficulty after a few weeks and Lóránt after several months.

Zoltán Czibor was persuaded not to leave on this occasion by his coach at Ferencváros, Antal Lyka, who pleaded with him that he and László Budai had been recruited in order to build a championship-winning team in 1949, the year of the club's 50th anniversary. Despite the imprisonment of a few first-team players, Ferencváros did just that.

Puskás had already been approached during Kispest's tour of Paris in 1947 but would tell anyone who listened during this time that he hadn't the slightest intention of signing abroad.

However, the temptation to escape a difficult societal situation must have been considerable. In the period after the war the situation was highly dangerous for his family, which was of Swabian descent – German, as far as most people were concerned, at a time when Hungarians of German heritage were being persecuted. The property of thousands of Hungarian Swabians was confiscated and they were relocated either to

Germany or to the Hungarian countryside amid wretched conditions. The regime's excuse for this collective punishment was the official line that they held the Swabians responsible for the war. Puskás believed this danger only ceased to exist for his family if he played football, and played well.

The first offer to tempt Puskás with an astronomical sum of money took place in 1947 and, no matter that many similar offers may have come later, he never forgot it. For as long as he lived he kept the written offer, in Hungarian, from the Hungarian representation of the FIAT factory, inviting him to Juventus. Puskás was 20 when the national team played Italy in Turin. There he made such an impact that Juventus began a courtship that continued long after the Hungarians returned home. They wanted to sign him at all costs. The document Puskás kept reveals that Juventus offered a flat, a car of his choosing, a signing-on fee of 40,000 Lira and a unique and astute proposition: Öcsi could take his father with him and they would immediately name him team coach.

Puskás alludes to this possibility in his 1955 autobiography, *Captain of Hungary*, making no secret of the fact that the temptation to accept tortured him and that he had many sleepless nights because of it. He finally decided to remain at the stadium across from his old family home in Kispest, where he had everything, and where he owed the supporters so much.

Even after the installation of the dictatorship, Puskás didn't want to defect for three basic reasons. Firstly, at this time there was a serious risk involved in defecting. An illegal attempt to cross the border was a crime which carried the death penalty. The wonderful Újpest central defender, Sándor Szűcs, was hanged in 1951 for his failed attempt. The second reason was that Puskás still continued to play well at home. He was immensely popular in Kispest. He helped the local community, the team was improving and the national team was becoming more successful than ever. Finally, he was not worldly. Puskás did not speak any foreign languages. He had such a good thing going in Hungary that he perhaps couldn't even imagine himself living abroad. The dictatorship turned him into an advertisement for the regime and did everything to increase his popularity. People worshipped him and, despite the gulf between his lifestyle in Budapest and that which he could expect in Turin or elsewhere, he wanted for little. However, as he saw life in Hungary change under the dictatorship, he began to become less settled. And when travelling abroad, it became apparent to him just how much more a footballer could earn – particularly if he was Ferenc Puskás.

REVOLUTION

THE PARLIAMENT buildings in Budapest are perched decorously on the banks of the Danube, their presence a tribute to the notion of democracy and the aesthetic of architecture. There is, though, another message that is enshrined in the very walls of surrounding buildings.

One can put one's finger in the bullet holes that testify powerfully that democracy has been hard won in Hungary and the battle for it was stained in blood.

Modern Budapest is a city that embraces the new-found freedom of a world that travels easily and endlessly to beautiful cities. Once, it was different.

Ferenc Puskás was brought up during a war that ended with a spasm of outrageous violence in the city. He knew of the threat of death, the reality of starvation and the necessity to endure.

The carve-up of Europe after the Second World War left Hungary in the hands of Joseph Stalin's Russia. The Hungary Puskás represented so brilliantly was part of the Soviet bloc.

This Hungary was condemned to a repressive communism that banned free speech, allowed corruption to flourish and even controlled football – aligning teams with organs of the state, and deciding which players joined which clubs.

The communist state under Mátyás Rákosi began a brutal series of purges and the imposition of economic plans that were simply unworkable and weakened the country.

The death of Stalin in 1953 and the denunciation of the dictator by Nikita Khrushchev, the Soviet leader, in February 1956 emboldened critics of the regime throughout the Eastern Bloc. Dissent grew in Budapest, most particularly among the students. Under pressure, Rákosi resigned. On October 23, 1956, more than 20,000 people gathered at a protest march in Budapest. Throughout the day, the crowd grew, reaching an estimated 200,000. The protest was brutally repressed with shots fired and many killed.

Soviet tanks were on the streets of Budapest the next morning and fighting broke out between Russian troops and poorly-armed but fervent Hungarian protesters. On October 30, in a lull in the fighting, the Soviet leaders issued a conciliatory statement. A peaceful solution seemed in sight with reforms promised. But on November 4 the Soviet leadership slammed its boot on the throat of Hungary. Soviet tanks re-entered the city, backed by a formidable force of troops. The resistance continued but was ultimately crushed. The communist rule of Hungary was reinforced. More than 200,000 Hungarians fled the country.

Puskás and his team-mates were abroad on tour throughout the fighting. The great footballer chose exile. It was a decision that caused him extraordinary problems for decades. He was given an army rank to play football for Honvéd, the army team, so his defection could be seen as desertion, and carry a death sentence.

The marvellous footballer celebrated from Madrid to Madras was condemned by authorities in Budapest, his every move criticised and questioned.

The author shows the Hungarian edition of this book to Puskás

Even as a baby, Puskás kept tight control of the ball

The emerging stars of Kispest FC. Puskás is third from right, his father is far left and Bozsik is on the left of the middle row

Puskás wins a header for Kispest, before his neighbourhood club changed their colours and their name on the order of the state

Puskás scores again – this time at the home of Ferencvaros, the Budapest giant eclipsed by Honvéd after the war

Puskás bought his parents a house from the money he made guesting for Ferencvaros on a tour of Mexico in 1947

The brand new Budapesti Honvéd, rebranded from Kispest FC as the army team.
Puskás holds the captain's pennant

Puskás during his legendary years at Honvéd

Unable to play through injury, Puskás is still the star attraction as Honvéd play in Italy during the 1956 tour

Puskás meets his public

The great József Bozsik catches up on some light reading in Stockholm in 1955

Bozsik, left, and Puskás, with a friend

Bozsik, Kocsis, Puskás and Lóránt edge their way through the crowd

Béla Guttman, Sándor Kocsis and Puskás discuss tactics

Puskás rises above the Czechoslovakia defence for Hungary

Puskás receives the gold medal for Hungary at the 1952 Helsinki Olympics

England 3 Hungary 6 – Puskás and Billy Wright lead out their respective teams in a match which would become one of the most defining of the 20th century

Puskás and Wright exchange gifts prior to kick off in 1954

Puskás and Wright leave the pitch after Hungary have beaten England 7–1 in Budapest

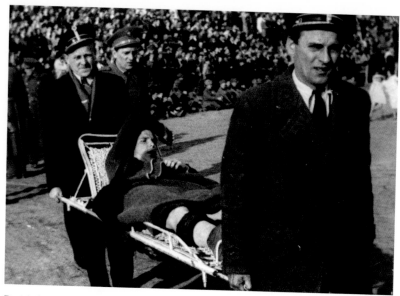

Puskás is stretchered off during the second half of Hungary's group game against West Germany in 1954

Puskás

Puskás earned his nickname 'The Galloping Major' from his time in the Hungarian army

Despite holding an army ranking, football always took priority in Puskás' life

Puskás of Madrid

Grosics, Puskás and Kocsis take a break after a training exhibition in Greece in 1957. 20,000 fans paid to see Puskás and Kocsis take pot shots at Grosics

Emil Östreicher, the man who negotiated Puskás' move to Real Madrid, with the Hungarian striker

A common sight – Puskás scores for Madrid

Puskás checks out the morning headlines during a walk in the mountains
outside Madrid

Puskás getting changed in the Real Madrid dressing room with Alfredo Di Stéfano

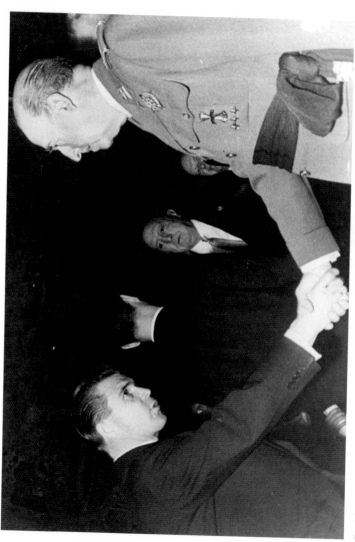

Puskás greets Spanish dictator General Franco, who ignored FIFA's ban and allowed Puskás to play for Madrid. Santiago Bernabéu is in the background

Puskás and The Animals – taking a different kind of shot

Real Madrid, season 1959-60. One of the greatest club sides ever assembled, including a lean, mean Puskás, second right, bottom row

Puskás with the European Cup, which he
won three times

Alfredo di Stéfano, Luis Suarez and Puskas, Spain team-mates at the 1962 World Cup

Puskás, Östreicher and Kubala

Puskás holds Helenio Herrera's daughter, as the Spain boss looks on with Joe Csabai, later Puskás' assistant coach in Vancouver

László Kubala, József Tóth-Zele and Puskás

Puskás puts his Panathinaikos players through their paces

Marshalling a practice session at Panathinaikos, with the help of his translator Nikos Sakoulis (No.6)

Puskás munches on sunflower seeds during a Panathinaikos match

1981 Upon his return to Hungary for the first time in 25 years, Puskás could still draw a crowd whenever he pulled on his boots

Cristiano Ronaldo, the inaugural winner of the FIFA Puskás award in 2009

Puskás' state funeral takes place in the national stadium which bears his name

Erzsébet Puskás shows the Hungarian version of the book to Sir Alex Ferguson

Puskás' footprint on the Champions Promenade in Monaco. A special plastercast was made of his feet in his hospital in Budapest

The hero of his age was portrayed as a traitor. Puskás felt the pain of this unjustified, politically inflicted wound throughout his life.

In the autumn of 1956, Hungary finally defeated the Soviets in Moscow and the Austrians in Vienna. Hungary won in Moscow with a shot in off the bar from Zoltán Czibor. "I shouted to Lev Yashin: 'Careful, watch your fingers!'" said the outside-left.

The national team coach Márton Bukovi had gone into the dressing room minutes before the final whistle and, hearing the din following a Soviet goal which was disallowed for offside, was certain the home team had equalised. "A draw in Moscow is a good result," he told the team when they returned to the dressing room.

Puskás replied: "But we won 1–0!"

"Oh, that's even better."

Meanwhile, in Czibor's hometown of Komárom, Russian soldiers from the nearby barracks were pelting his parents' house with stones.

Shortly afterwards, the national team was in the Hungarian town of Tata preparing for a match in Budapest against Sweden (the Under-23 team was already abroad and were playing England in London when the Uprising broke out in Hungary. The bulk of this outstanding team remained abroad afterwards). Here, on October 23, the players listened to the radio and, although for a while they convinced themselves they should stay and train, it soon dawned on them that there could hardly be a match on the Sunday in the Népstadion.

At the beginning of the Uprising György Szepesi[14] was still conducting a desperate appeal on the radio to the public:

14   a Hungarian radio personality, journalist and sports administrator)

"Comrades, go home so it will be possible to organise the match!"

From Czibor's diary at the time of the Uprising I know that the players arranged a train for themselves which would take them from the station beside the training camp to Kelenföld station in Budapest, from where Puskás and the others would later go home to their families.

On the morning of November 1, 1956, the Honvéd bus left for Vienna. The aim was that the team should be able to prepare for their European Cup match against Athletic Bilbao. The tournament was in its second year, and the first leg, in Bilbao, was to take place on November 22.

During the Uprising, the team elected a revolutionary committee, of which Zoltán Czibor was to be head and, as such, he allowed a military leader to stay on the player's bus. The bus left, with some of the players' wives anxiously bidding them farewell, not realising that some of them were now leaving on a much longer journey.

In Komárom, they stopped off at the house of one of Czibor's relatives for food. At that time he didn't consider dropping in on his parents, a couple of blocks away, saying: "I'll be back in a few weeks, so let's not waste time with farewells."

Those few weeks became 27 years. In Komárom today you can walk down Czibor utca.

News spread in Western Europe that Puskás had died during the fighting in Budapest. In the archives of *La Dernière Heures* in Brussels I found a typed report prepared in Paris on October 27, according to which the famous Hungarian footballer Ferenc Puskás had been killed in Budapest: "The Hungarian Puskás, captain of the national football team, who fought on the side of the insurrectionists, may have been killed in Budapest." A similar notice appeared in *Marca*, in Madrid.

Within a few days the rumours appeared all over the world, after which others appeared saying that the Budapest Honvéd team had crossed the Austrian-Hungarian border. Puskás remembered that the border guards were shocked when they saw him on the bus among the others, since they already believed he was dead.

At the time of leaving, some of the Hungarian players touring in the West had already hesitated over whether they should take their wives and indeed a few days later – on hearing the news from home of the street battles and the Soviet intervention – the footballers were overcome with worry. There were those who spent all their money on telephone calls home and as it became obvious that the situation was unstable and dangerous, the majority of them began to arrange how to get their families across the border. In these days of fighting and uncertainty, well-organised groups worked on arranging defection to Austria – for good money. The players, using the contacts they had developed during their smuggling days, tried to arrange their business through the main Viennese contact, Sándor Schwartz. They paid him and those working for him around $2000 for each person they wanted to bring out from Hungary.

However, getting people out of revolutionary Hungary was not as easy as getting watches in under the dictatorship. Not all of the escapees made it across undetected. At such times they were arrested and sent back to Budapest, or prison in Győr.

Puskás' wife, Erzsébet, had tried and failed twice to leave before she eventually got out. The previous night in a school gym hall, a group of players' families were laying low. Zoltán Czibor's young son was given brandy in order to better handle the final hours before their escape. But because of this he just got louder.

Erzsébet told me how she and her daughter, the then four

year-old Anikó, crossed the by-then closed border at the end of November. This time she set off with only her daughter and the wife of the Honvéd doctor Tamás Fried, as members of a larger group. The story is told here by Erzsébet:

"It's interesting, I remember that I never spoke directly with Öcsi on the phone about it – I always only received messages from him. One time, just after we'd got home from another unsuccessful escape attempt, I got a message.

We met with them outside. We went with the doctor's wife. We went by train. The person we went with said that the train would slow down at a village called Levél, and that we had to jump off there. With the children – you can imagine. We went into the village, hiding from tree to tree. I think anyone could have seen us if they'd wanted to, but at that time all we knew was that we had to hide.

We then arrived at a house. We had to go in. In the house we waited for a man; he'd said that we must wait until dark. After dusk we started on our way. With my first step I crashed into a large ditch – forwards, then back. There were more of us than when we'd started off – they came from other places and joined up with us. Our leader stayed with us for a while then left us to ourselves to carry on to the Austrian border.

After a time, I remember beginning to have misgivings that perhaps we weren't heading in the right direction. Naturally I didn't say who I was – I didn't reveal it to anyone, God forbid. In every group there is someone whose brain works better than the others' and such a person said, under their breath, that they had the feeling we should go in another direction, but according to another in our group, yet another direction was correct.

We split into two groups, everyone went with their gut feeling. This was when we parted company from the doctor's wife and her daughter. We got lost and weren't able to say anything. Thank God they also got out afterwards – her husband became a famous doctor in America and we wrote to each other for a long time.

This was the end of November. There was mud everywhere. A woman put her coat around Anikó. She was four. I carried her until a young man took mercy on me and carried her for me, but I constantly held her arm so I didn't lose her. I had put a piece of paper in each of her pockets, on to which I wrote her name and personal details, in case we lost each other somehow. My God…

I only took a small bag, a bottle of water, a few family pictures and my most valued jewellery. Someone offered to help by carrying my bag for me, but I've never seen it since then. One time we came up against something huge. The men decided that it was a large haystack. There seemed no end to it, it was so long, so big. I didn't know how to get around it. We climbed up to the top of it and, helping each other, slid down. Afterwards we said that if it was a haystack we should get into it and rest until daybreak – until we could finally see something. We had walked for hours. I lost my shoes in the mud and found them only after kneeling down on all fours. Drenched, I tried to warm up Anikó. She had problems with her kidneys for a while afterwards – Anikó doesn't remember anything of the whole story. She behaved very well on this adventure. She whispered: 'Mum! When will we get there?'

'Soon,' I always answered. I told her when we set off that we were going to Dunaföldvár to see her godmother.

Somewhere in the distance a light shone. We set off towards it in the hope that something would be there. We didn't think – at that time people go with half of their minds and don't even know what they're doing. But we didn't have any other choice. We had to set off for somewhere. Soon we found a small house.

There wasn't a soul around but then a man saw something on the ground. He picked it up and began to look at it. It was a cartridge box, written in German.

'We're in Austria!' he shouted. It was freezing, my God. We hugged each other.

Afterwards we started on the road. I tied my hair in plaits. All of us were covered in mud. A horse-drawn cart came and the driver shouted, 'Come on! I'll take you to Nickelsdorf!'

We then went to a beautiful cottage – after the greyness of Hungary it was like a mansion to us! The locals received us kindly and all around us the women immediately set about cooking. From here we were taken to the Green Cross refugee camp. There, we received piping hot cocoa and were taken to a huge container full with clothes so we could change out of our muddy things. I got a large pair of men's socks and a small pair of shoes. I had to tread on the heels but I was happy that it was finally warm.

We stood in line. Everyone had to fill in a form. The woman who was there stopped at my name and immediately spoke with someone, at which point they took me and my daughter in a separate car to Vienna, to the Münchendorf Hotel. They also took the man who had carried Anikó and who after a while had said "sorry, I can't go any further, I only have one lung". He would have been around 18 – all I know is that he was trying to get to a relative in Italy who had an antique business. He was still with us in Vienna. After that he didn't appear again. I always waited for him to turn up[15]

We were taken into a room in the hotel with Anikó. There was a sofa where this boy was resting and the bathroom was outside in the corridor. I was with Anikó, the two of us in the bed, under a feather eiderdown. The feeling I had there ... I clutched Anikó to myself.

I received a message that I shouldn't show myself in the hotel since it would harm the chances of those who still hadn't been able to get out. I laid low for this reason. I escaped downstairs just the once,

---

15   *The young man who carried Anikó was Thomas Csonka. Later, while living in Switzerland, he read of Anikó's death in Spain and wrote to the Puskás Academy website, telling of his involvement in the family's escape. He was reunited with Erzsébet in Budapest in 2013.*

when the Bild photographer pictured me. Years later I received that newspaper from someone. Even later, I heard that the radio had already announced a while before that we had arrived.

Sándor Kocsis' wife Aliz, and daughter, arrived shortly after. Aliz said that Sanyi [Sándor Kocsis] was coming for us. But from where? I didn't know. Since then I haven't found out, either. I didn't speak about this with anyone. The point is that Sanyi came for us and took us to Milan and then left us there. The wives assembled in Milan while the men played matches in all sorts of places. I first sat on an aeroplane then – it was as if I'd gone from nothing to the whole thing being a fairytale.

But it's not such a special story; countless Hungarians lived through this. Well, this is how we got out. We were young, we didn't sense the danger. On the other hand, we'd lived through the war, the bombings, and the regime. I said at that time that I never wanted to go home ever again."

Earlier, on November 1, the Honvéd players left by bus, with permits. What's more, the new Prime Minister Imre Nagy sent a message for the departing sportsmen that read: 'We've already won our [home] match – now you win abroad.'

Czibor procured papers during the days of the Uprising and the team prepared to travel, with proper passports and permits, from in front of the Budapest Honvéd headquarters on Dózsa György út. The same is not entirely true about the players joining later. Gyula Grosics in Tatabánya for example, was taken by an army truck to the border, his plane ticket to Madrid already awaiting him in Vienna, after it emerged that the Honvéd squad needed a goalkeeper. That same evening he kept goal in a match against a Real/Atlético select team which finished 5-5, a game organised for charity to help the Hungarian refugees on the initiative of General Franco's wife.

Honvéd had left so they could prepare for the European Cup match at the end of November against Bilbao. Puskás' team lost the first leg 3-2 in the Basque country, however, it did not enter their minds to return home. Indeed, by then the situation in Hungary had become even more dangerous: many had died during ongoing fighting, there had been thousands of escapees and the future outcome was still far from certain. The date of the return leg was approaching and UEFA didn't approve of them playing the match in Budapest, which had been swept into a war-like situation. If the players must remain abroad to play, it was reasonable for their families to join them.

Brussels on December 20 was set as the match venue. Between the two European Cup matches, Honvéd played in Spain (5-5 against the Madrid select, 4-3 against Barcelona, 2-6 against Sevilla), in Italy (Milan 2-1, Roma 2-3, Palermo 6-2, Palermo select 7-1, Catania 9-2), and en-route in West Germany (Werder Bremen 4-1); for the most part in front of 40- or 50,000 spectators.

The former national team coach Gusztáv Sebes travelled to Brussels for the second leg with the aim of persuading the team to return home and restoring the national team of its stars. The team received him respectfully in Brussels, but when he petitioned the players to leave for home immediately after the match, Czibor rebuked him by saying: "Leave it out, Oldie!"

Sebes primarily tried to persuade Puskás. He thought it all depended on the captain. Öcsi, however, didn't emphasise his own point of view, rather the decision which the team had already voted for – that they would next travel to South America, from where they had received a tempting offer. Puskás staved off Sebes' advances by personally guaranteeing the return of the whole team if they received an official permit from the MLSZ for the South American tour. Öcsi even invited

Gusztáv Sebes to stay with the team. He declined the invitation and travelled home despondently with minimal success, having only persuaded a few young players to accompany him back to Hungary. Honvéd, meanwhile, drew 3-3 with Bilbao and with this were knocked out of the European Cup. According to some, they didn't really want to go through, since progression in the European Cup would have put the lucrative and exciting tour in danger.

Instead they returned to their permanent base in Italy, where their wives and children awaited them. Europe burned in the fever of the Hungarian Uprising and everyone was watching Budapest. There were daily updates across international media on the fight for freedom in Hungary and Europe-wide protests of solidarity broke out in front of Hungarian embassies. Around this time, Albert Camus wrote beautifully about the Hungarian Uprising. Honvéd then went on their tour of South America, but FIFA began to make threats to the South American national associations so that they wouldn't dare allow any more matches against the dissident team to take place. Finally the Hungarian and international federation achieved their goal. Under the weight of these threats, South American teams refused to arrange any more matches with Honvéd. In addition, the atmosphere within the team became heavier. The players had been locked up together for four months without family members, and even the best relationships were being eroded. Above all, everyone had reason to worry about their fate. Those returning home feared the punishment awaiting them and perhaps the feeling of regret at missing a great opportunity. Those staying abroad had to confront the uncertainty of their future and the terrible homesickness. In the dressing room after one of the defeats, Czibor supposedly accused Bozsik of sabotaging the match because he was a communist. A fight nearly broke out, so strained were the players' nerves.

At the beginning of February it became obvious that they needed to return to Europe. This wasn't straightforward because firstly visas needed to be acquired. The citizens of the communist country residing abroad without permits, who a few months ago had been welcomed with open arms and accepted as political refugees by the Western world, weren't able to return back at whichever moment they chose. They went from door to door at South American embassies, composed travel plans and waited for official papers. Finally, at various intervals, they travelled back via Holland or Spain to Vienna, where their wives were waiting. Eleven players went back to Budapest within two days, where they were let off with relatively short bans. Puskás, Czibor, Kocsis and Grosics all stayed in Vienna.

If earlier in their careers, the members of the *Aranycsapat* had resisted lucrative offers at least in part due to their belief that theirs was a golden era, defeat in the World Cup final of 1954 had altered the collective mood. The footballers sensed their era would one day end and they would be left to raise their families with whatever they had saved from their football careers.

In this atmosphere, the Hungarian Uprising occurred, and amid its darkness and uncertainty, the wealthy football clubs of Europe focused their attentions on the Hungarians as never before. While the dispute over permission for the tour carried on and the messages arrived imploring them to return home, Emil Östreicher wrote a letter to Sándor Barcs, president of MLSZ, and the director of the MTI[16] in which he laid bare the discrepancy between how much a Honvéd player could earn in Hungary and in the West, and then put the question: "What do you think they should do?"

---

16   Magyar Távirati Iroda – the Hungarian News Agency

Barcs, of course, couldn't respond, not even in Vienna, to where the MLSZ delegation travelled in an attempt to order the team home. The negotiating delegation didn't promise any increase in the payments made to the footballers, or the cancelling of the promised ban awaiting them upon their return. Puskás only said that they should think it over, speak with those back in Hungary and see what was possible, since if they really did ban him for a year, as they had promised, he certainly wouldn't go home. The delegation would not move: Puskás had to be heavily reprimanded since as team captain he bore great responsibility for the organisation of the team's illegal South American tour. Therefore, Puskás confirmed he would not return.

Puskás repeatedly mentioned later that he remained abroad because he had been accused of something he hadn't done, something which made him bitter and angry. What was the accusation he had in mind? Perhaps, that they hung the organisation of the South American tour around his neck, whereas in reality the players had decided for themselves who would or wouldn't go to Brazil.

Öcsi may have been thinking about articles that appeared in the press accusing him of swindling his team-mates. This was a terrible accusation and since then the charge has been denied by all those who could, something which may have dissipated Puskás' outrage.

Many swear that the last straw was a newspaper article which ended up in Puskás' hands in Vienna. Here Puskás, apparently writing in the first person, explained why he was staying abroad, listing mostly political reasons and criticising communism. He was still protesting in vain decades later that he never said such things. Indeed, he never would engage in politics. Or become a gangster – but that didn't stop another article during the early years of his exile claiming that Puskás was a Mafia boss who led half the underworld.

THE FOOTBALLER IN EXILE

THE HUNGARIAN UPRISING was the single pivotal point in the life of Ferenc Puskás. Many people who knew him say that if Puskás had not remained in the West after 1956, if destiny hadn't compelled him to a life immeasurably different from his previous one, then the idolised and pampered star would soon have retired. Instead, he started a new and at least as successful career. The outcome was that Puskás wouldn't just remain a part of history as the greatest Hungarian footballer that ever lived, but also as arguably the best player in the world. Ferenc Puskás' metamorphosis after 1956 is inspirational and still unbelievable to this day.

Puskás lived for most of 1957 under terrible uncertainty and with heavy responsibility on his shoulders. It had already been decided that he wouldn't be going home. No one knew what would be waiting for him, and he couldn't live where people spread such falsehoods about him.

However, his future was uncertain. The communists did all they could to persuade FIFA to extend bans on defecting players. Their endeavours found success and the appetite of the teams interested in signing Puskás vanished, as no club wanted to pay the wages of a footballer who couldn't play. The ban was so strict that the Hungarian players who had left their country were theoretically forbidden from even training on any football pitch in the world.

At the end of February 1957 the players arrived back in Vienna from the South American tour, where they were reunited with their families. Here, Puskás met with a Hungarian federation delegation which summoned him home, but warned he would receive the most severe punishment of all the players – a year's ban. Puskás asked the delegation to reconsider but the next day their response was the same. He therefore came to the hardest and most important decision of his life: he would not return home to Hungary.

He remained in the West without a word of Italian, English or German. Without professional football, he began to put on weight. An ageing footballer – in April 1957 he was already over 30 – with no other career skills, responsible for his family in a new, unknown world from which the road home had been closed, seemingly forever.

From here, he travelled to Italy. The area beside Sanremo was familiar – he had trained here with the national team. Now Puskás trained alone, each morning on the nearby club pitch, in an anxious mood.

For a short while it seemed as if he would sign for the Austrian club Wiener SC; they concluded an agreement with Emil Östreicher, who was working in Vienna as he began his own new life away from Hungary. However, the FIFA ban remained.

There were only occasional matches organised with the participation of the large number of exiled Hungarians. Once, in Greece, Puskás, Grosics and Kocsis trained in front of a stadium of 10,000 paying spectators. This group was called the Puskás Circus. These tours also slowly came to an end though.

FIFA imposed strict sanctions on any club that spoke to the banned Hungarians and the players couldn't even play under aliases as members of teams with mixed nationalities.

Puskás' problem seemed to be resolved when, towards the end of the ban, Internazionale of Milan offered him a pre-contract. But the clubs had to register their signed players before the start of the season and at that time, Puskás was still banned.

His next offer was to coach, rather than play, for a club in Portugal. Puskás was furious. He was determined that he could still play at the top of the sport.

In 1958, serious negotiations between Puskás and Manchester United broke down. Maximum wage regulations were in place in Britain, and a footballer's earning was capped at £18-per-week. As well as Puskás, the English club also met with Kocsis and Czibor, but United couldn't reach any kind of compromise with FIFA. The Old Trafford faithful only had the opportunity to see Puskás once, in 1959, when Madrid made a charity appearance in aid of the Munich Disaster fund and beat their hosts 6-1. Puskás played for the visitors, and not for £18, but instead for around £800 a week.

Puskás was beset by financial worries in 1957. Practically all his money was invested in a house in the Zugló district of Budapest and, moreover, a few payments were still outstanding. While the tour matches paid well, his income was erratic while his life was pretty expensive. Everyone expected something from him: he was expected to shine and help his fellow countrymen who had stumbled on hard times, and he always did. In his first period in Vienna, according to the great Honvéd goalkeeper Lajos Faragó, Puskás allotted around $5000 to those who asked him for help, whether he knew them or not. Puskás would reach into his pockets and slip $100 or $200 into the other person's hand and tell them: "Off you go – don't let me see you again!"

He was also cared for by László Kubala. He was born in the same district of Budapest and in the same year as Puskás and was already a superstar in Barcelona, having fled Hungary in the back of a truck when the communists took power in 1949. Before that the two had played together in a Budapest youth team, in 1941, and again during Kubala's brief, three-match career as a Hungary international, either side of which he represented Czechoslovakia and Spain.

Not only did he know Puskás, he had a good idea of what he was going through and loaned him money. As Erzsébet later said: "Kubala was a king in Catalonia and he was a king in our lives, too."

Why did FIFA punish the Hungarian players so severely? Within FIFA there were a similar amount of representatives from the communist countries as there were for the Western ones but the former were at least as influential and certainly more united and determined. For these Eastern-Bloc associations it was a question of vital importance that they should hit the defecting players with heavy sanctions. If this didn't happen, the fall-out would threaten socialist sport and every elite sportsman and woman would leave at the first given opportunity.

This was a stressful period in Puskás' life. He suffered a serious gastric haemorrhage at the time. With this ulcer, his uncertainty of existence, the loss of his home environment and carrying excess weight, only the 30-year-old Puskás trusted himself to be a footballer again. And perhaps Emil Östreicher.

PUSKÁS OF MADRID

'Bernabéu wants you'

EMIL ÖSTREICHER was his saviour. Östreicher had been Honvéd's financial secretary and was with the squad when they left Hungary. While the 'Puskás Cricus' moved around Europe and club after club considered and then declined to oppose the FIFA ban, Östreicher was able to adapt far more quickly. After a brief stop at Wiener SC – where he was behind the nascent attempt to recruit Puskás – he received an offer that would change his life, and that of his close friend, the exiled captain of Hungary.

Östreicher was multilingual and confident and had built a reputation within elite football from taking the Honvéd team around Europe. They had caused a sensation in Madrid, where Östreicher had met with Real president Santiago Bernabéu. This led to an offer to advise Bernabéu at Madrid, and his first piece of guidance for the president was that he should sign the best footballer in the world. But Bernabéu wasn't a fan of the idea. He didn't have good memories of Puskás.

Bernabéu saw Puskás play in his penultimate match for the Hungarian national team against France in Paris in October

1956 and didn't fancy the Galloping Major at all. Puskás played terribly and a consensus was forming that he was on his way down. He had put on weight, he was short of pace, he had become pampered and had aged. What Bernabéu liked even less was that Puskás complained to and constantly argued with the referee. This was enormously important for the president. He did not want a troublemaker.

Östreicher, however, had seen the best of Puskás, and was convinced that the great forward was not finished yet. He lobbied the president hard. Bernabéu relented: "Okay, let's see what he can do and then we'll consider it."

Östreicher flew off to Milan. He was to scout Real's next European Cup opponents, but his most important goal was clandestine – to tell Puskás: "My dear Öcsi, Bernabéu wants you." Puskás was on the verge of giving up playing when he heard from Östreicher. When they met, his old friend drew up a plan to prepare Puskás – out of shape and almost without hope – for his big opportunity.

It has been said that Bernabéu began to pay Puskás without having seen him and later became unwell when he saw how overweight the Hungarian was. The president had requested an immediate meeting with his new recruit. "I looked like a giant balloon," remembered Puskás.

Puskás now had to lose weight. "My willpower was as strong as three elephants," he said. He gave up his excessive eating and drinking. He wrapped himself in nylon and ran almost from morning until night. He said: "I knew I was able to play football and that I'd score goals for Real Madrid. I believed in myself. I believed in my ability."

He lost 18 kilograms. He became fitter, and was more experienced and more ambitious than ever. He was ready to amaze the world once again.

His challenge was not only physical, but political. Puskás, by now already 31 years old, came under the management of a coach who hated him. The conflict began before their first meeting. When word broke of Öcsi's contract with Madrid, head coach Luis Antonio Carniglia announced to Östreicher that he had no need for Puskás.

"He's not even a footballer," said the coach.

Östreicher replied: "You've never seen a footballer such as Puskás."

After he arrived, many Madrid training sessions would consist of the others practising with the ball while Puskás had to run round and round the pitch.

'Puskás is not for sale at any price'

They say that in the beginning, the genius of the team, Alfredo Di Stéfano called his new team-mate 'fatso'. Di Stéfano said he did not understand what his world-beating Madrid wanted with a player fit only for an old boys' team. The many assists received from Puskás slowly gave him the answer to his questions. It was the start of a partnership which would become legendary.

Puskás played and scored goals in the first year, although it wasn't easy to assimilate. The club loaned him out to their city rivals Atlético, with the not-so-secret aim that Atlético would offer him the opportunity to play, place him in the shop window and find a buyer for him. Their coup in bringing Puskás back would be used as a mere business opportunity.

In spite of these slights, Puskás didn't become disheartened, but instead worked even harder. He played so well on loan at Atlético that president Bernabéu changed his point of view, saying: "Puskás is not for sale at any price."

By now the president was on Puskás' side. His unrivalled

determination had slowly won round his many doubters, with one exception. Carniglia remained opposed to Puskás, but when the two crossed paths again, it was the coach who was ousted from Madrid.

Puskás had been playing wonderfully throughout the spring of 1959, but was left out of the team for the European Cup final of that year by Carniglia, who said the Hungarian player was injured. Puskás knew nothing about any injury – only that he was being denied the chance to play in the European Cup final for the first time in his career. He could not have known he would become so familiar with the occasion.

The final was played in June 1959 in Stuttgart, West Germany. Puskás watched from the stands. During the game Bernabéu asked him why he wasn't playing. Puskás answered that perhaps the president should ask his coach. Puskás recalled that Bernabéu didn't say anything at the time (the team won the match 2-0 against Stade de Reims to secure their fourth European title, and the second under Carniglia) but at the start of the new season the president introduced a new coach to the dressing room, Manuel Fleitas. He had sacked Carniglia, two-time winner of the European Cup. One year later Puskás repaid Bernabéu's faith by playing the lead role in another European Cup final – the most famous of them all.

Puskás received Spanish citizenship very quickly. All who escaped to Spain recall that the embassy of the Hungarian monarchy still operated in the country, long after being overthrown in Budapest. While communist Hungary did not have diplomatic relations with Franco's Spain, the Hungarian royal embassy was still recognised. The Puskás family received their first official papers from here, soon after which most Hungarian footballers who applied also received Spanish citizenship. A maximum of two foreigners could appear for

Spanish clubs, so citizenship made a huge difference to the footballers. One player said it was a straightforward matter to achieve Spanish citizenship. They were summoned before General Franco, who would sign the papers and say: "OK guys, just don't be communists."

So it was that Spain accepted and treated as assets Zoltán Czibor, Sándor Kocsis and Ferenc Puskás, three of the greatest gems of the *Aranycsapat*. Other countries where clubs had approached the exiled Hungarians – Italy, Austria, Switzerland and England – either felt the influence of FIFA and its 'Eastern wing' or could not offer professional terms.

Politically, Franco naturally didn't have any qualms with those who had left communism. Moreover, in terms of the politics of sport, Spanish football already existed as an independent world with its own laws. While the Spanish national team was incapable of achieving any kind of international success in the late 1950s, Spanish clubs were continually among the world's best. In Spain, football primarily means club football or, to be more exact, Real Madrid and Barcelona. The two clubs exert nearly as much influence over its people as a state might. Why was this important from Puskás' perspective? Spain was probably the market capable of paying the most and wasn't in the least concerned with FIFA.

In Spain, Czibor and Puskás began training before their bans expired and they even received money from their clubs. When someone put the question to Franco that Spain could be expelled from FIFA if they gave a playing opportunity and livelihood to the banned Hungarians, the dictator replied: "What's FIFA?"

Real Madrid offered a generous four-year contract. For his signature, Puskás received $25,000 in advance. On top of this there was a monthly wage of $3500 dollars as well as a bonus which, considering that Real won most of their matches, worked out at around the same amount again.

As Östreicher put it: "It wasn't an astronomical amount for Real, but for the podgy Puskás this counted as really good money."

He felt drawn towards football like never before. The game had always been at the centre of his life but here he learned to really appreciate his talent.

In Budapest, legends still circulate about him being sent on to the pitch in a league match while hungover, scoring two first-half goals and then, having asked permission, returning to the dressing room to sleep. Here at Real Madrid this was unimaginable. He had to keep his new figure, acquired by hard work, and for this he needed to show unprecedented discipline. He stayed away from snacks and alcohol, he became accustomed to fish and light foods and despite the late nights customary to Spanish life, was reluctant to stay up after midnight.

Puskás had discovered a second career at the elite level, and he knew the clock was ticking on his ability as a footballer. If he had to adjust his lifestyle to remain a part of Madrid's successes, then that is what he would do. Sándor Barcs even noted in his book, published in the 1960s, that when he'd been invited to dinner he didn't recognize this Puskás who drank mineral water and ate seafood. To Barcs' amazement, Öcsi responded: "I'm a professional here and I have to take care of myself."

From one of the greatest virtuoso footballing characters, a purposeful professional emerged. Károly 'Csikar' Sándor, after whom the MTK Budapest football club's academy in Agárd is named, was a great admirer of Puskás. For years they played cards, fooled around at national team get-togethers and, of course, played and won together. Csikar insisted many times that he held a higher opinion of Puskás than he did of all the others because he showed he could rise again after 1956.

"If Öcsi had stayed at home he would have left football. I'm sure about this. He was overweight and playing poorly in relation to what he had been capable of. I was an eyewitness of this on the occasion of our victory in Paris a full two weeks before the Uprising. On the way home at the station – we travelled by train – the head coach Márton Bukovi reprimanded him. It began as a simple discussion but Bukovi worked himself up into a frenzy, in the end chastising Puskás exasperatedly. 'Are you not ashamed of yourself?' at which point Puskás burst into tears. We'd never seen anything like this from Öcsi before."

Now Puskás had to do everything humbly, without a glimmer of self-importance. It was imperative to gain the goodwill of Di Stéfano in order to gain his help. Decades later, when I tracked down Don Alfredo in Madrid, he characterised Puskás thus: "As a player and as a man, ten out of ten. He was a fantastic player and a wonderfully good man."

Alfredo himself later admitted thinking: 'What's this fatso doing here? Are they having a laugh?' when he first saw Puskás on the pitch, but soon he discovered that if Puskás shouted 'Stefi', he only had to stretch out his leg to find the ball arriving exactly where he wanted it. Furthermore, there is a splendid story of how Puskás was accepted once and for all by Di Stéfano. It was round 28 of the 1958-59 season in a game against Sevilla. Madrid were cruising, Puskás and Di Stéfano had already scored two goals each. That kept the Argentine top of the list for the Pichichi, the top goalscorer in the Spanish league. One ahead of Puskás.

In the 90th minute Puskás found himself in a goalscoring position. If he'd scored he'd have pulled level with Di Stéfano but instead he looked up, passed to Alfredo and shouted "finish it Stefi!" Neither of them scored in the final two rounds of the league, and so Di Stéfano finished Puskás' first season at Madrid as the league's top goalscorer, the last of his five Pichichi wins. Puskás would win the title in four of the next five seasons.

Of course, not everyone saw Puskás as a rival when he arrived at Real. The Frenchman Raymond Kopa, for example, revealed that he almost felt as if God had descended to earth. With the bonus he received for winning the French league as a young striker at Stade de Reims, Kopa had paid for a trip to London to see 'The Match of the Century'. From then on, Puskás was his footballing hero.

Kopa could scarcely have known that president Bernabéu had originally wanted to sign the Hungarian Károly Sándor in his position, only for the MTK outside-right and Puskás' age-old friend to consider living abroad unthinkable.

'I felt his stomach once and it was as hard as this table'

Alfredo Di Stéfano is waiting for me. We are at the headquarters of Real Madrid's veterans' team, a separate section in the huge Estadio Santiago Bernabéu with its own reception, office, club room and trophy room. Former players can come here anytime, arrange club afternoons and events and pour a drink for themselves from the bar. An initially moody Don Alfredo begins to relax and tell stories.

"I knew Gyula Zsengellér[17] too. I played in the same championship with him in Colombia. What a footballer he was! He told me that he gave the assist for Puskás' first goal in the national team.

Oh yes, I'd heard a lot already about the young Puskás before we became team-mates. But listen, there was a Hungarian forward

---

17   *Legendary Újpest FC and Hungary striker of the 1930s and 40s*

in Colombia, I can't remember his name, but he was a bit of a lad, a wide boy. He married a Colombian coffee baron's daughter and then their daughter was later crowned Miss Colombia. I read it. Oh, yes, these Hungarians were everywhere, and Pancho [Puskás] was always looking for their company, he helped them in any way possible – he would spend his money on them – on the Hungarians, as if he was the Hungarian Embassy!

Was he fat? Well, his build was somewhat stocky but he wasn't overweight. He was a ball of muscle. I felt his stomach once and it was as hard as this table.

Pancho was very quick, explosive. He outpaced everyone over ten metres. He had a wonderful technical knowledge and his passes and one-twos – he was a complete player, I think he would have played well in any position.

He was always cheerful and joking and perpetually in a good mood. He drank wine with soda water. This was unusual for us but he liked it that way. Always just white wine though. He would drink a little, and then pour a litre of soda water into a few decilitres of wine. Pancho paid a lot of attention to himself and how he looked.

How is Pancho? When did you last speak with his wife?"

"The president is waiting for you!" says Emilio Butragueño's secretary after we finish talking with Di Stéfano.

Florentino Pérez, the immensely rich building contractor and president of Real Madrid, welcomes us in a conspicuously luxurious conference room in his company's offices. The boss of possibly the world's most popular club found half an hour for us because of Ferenc Puskás' name.

"In my childhood I went to Real Madrid's matches with my father. I was 11 when Ferenc Puskás signed for us and 19 when he finished playing football at Real. So I'm not talking through my hat when I

say he was a genius of a personality in the club's history. I saw with my eyes from week to week the wonderful football that he paraded in front of us with Di Stéfano, Gento and the others.

Puskás took the free-kicks and penalties. He could shoot frighteningly well. I remember this most clearly. It's true he didn't run when he didn't need to. He didn't run a lot, but it wasn't his job. His job was to score goals and set them up for his team-mates.

Today's 'Madridism' was established by the football of Puskás and his colleagues. Puskás wasn't only a brilliant footballer but a gentleman who accepted defeat as graciously as victory. The requirements of 'Madridism' – the culture of Real Madrid – are the following: respect for the opponent; solidarity; the ability to battle; to lead and to be a gentleman. He perfectly suited all these.

When I applied for the president's position for the first time in 1995 he helped my campaign. He sometimes appeared with me and supported me in the press. I met him more often and can only confirm what I'd heard earlier about him from others – that he is a nice man with a good sense of humour. I've never heard a bad word about Puskás."

To help me understand the mystique around the No.10 shirt at Real, Florentino Pérez told a story. In his election campaign, Pérez memorably promised to bring Luis Figo from Barcelona to Real Madrid, something which may have in part helped to elect him. "Prior to Puskás' arrival the No.10 shirt didn't have any lustre or extra significance. It just meant that the person who played in that shirt was the inside-left. But since Puskás it means something else entirely. When Figo signed for us and he took the number, I told him: 'Forever wear this Real No.10 shirt in the way Puskás did.'"

Pérez named the European Cup final in Glasgow in 1960 as Puskás' most famous and most memorable match for Real

Madrid. "My father was there. At that time he travelled regularly with his friends to matches. As fate would have it I went as president to Glasgow where Real again played there in the final [against Bayer Leverkusen in the 2002 UEFA Champions League final]. I last met with Puskás there."

REAL MADRID 7
EINTRACHT FRANKFURT 3

European Cup final,
May 18 1960

IT was the match that brought the European Cup to the world. There can be arguments about some aspects of the arithmetic. Some say there were 127,000 people inside Hampden. Others insist 134,000. If one consults with natives of Glasgow, then one could be forgiven for suspecting that every man of a certain age attended, making the attendance run into seven figures instead of merely six. One confirmed spectator was a young footballer, then playing for Queen's Park, called Alex Ferguson.

There can be more certainty about the score and the significance of the match. Real Madrid defeated Eintracht Frankfurt 7-3, winning their fifth consecutive European Cup.

But it was Hampden 1960, captured in grainy black-and-white film, which hailed the greatest club side that had ever been seen. There had been scepticism in Britain about the worth of the European Cup, there was suspicion about the foreign game and how resilient it would be in the face of the more physical British game.

Any doubts about Madrid were swept away in the tumult of a packed and raucous Hampden. Frankfurt, who beat a strong Rangers side 12-4 over two legs in the semi-finals, were simply crushed by Real.

The swagger, the almost causal arrogance can be wondered at even now. Yes, the game was slower then. Yes, there was more space for forwards to exploit. But Real managed to make a European Cup final seem like an exhibition match.

The names are burned into the minds of anyone who was there, anyone who claims they were there and those who admit they merely watched film of the match. There was Canario, there was Luis Del Sol, there was Francisco Gento and there was Alfredo Di Stéfano. There was, most conspicuously, Ferenc Puskás. The Galloping Major scored four goals. Two years later he scored another hat-trick in a European Cup final. Only two other players – Di Stéfano (also in the Hampden final) and Pierino Prati – have scored hat-tricks in European Cup finals in the history of a tournament that stretches back to 1955.

But it was not a matter of statistics that enthralled the crowd. It was the sight of players who could do anything, everything and seemed determined to cram this into 90 minutes.

Puskás was to the fore. There were reports before the match that he had to apologise to the football authorities over his claims that the West German side had taken illegal drugs to win the 1954 World Cup final against Hungary.

Any contrition was followed by condign punishment on the German club side. Puskás was irresistible. His first-half goal, a left-shot of wicked venom, could serve as an emblem for his career, if there were not so many examples of that manoeuvre to choose from.

This, at the age of 33, was his greatest game. Puskás, was more fluid yet more powerful in his movement than ever before – he only used one or two touches at a time and was ruthlessly incisive and efficient in the build-up to the goals.

The match was broadcast almost everywhere in Europe except Hungary, where the communists would not show it for fear of aggrandising the escapee and 'traitor' Puskás.

Nevertheless, some enterprising Hungarians near the Austrian border made makeshift television antennas in order to access reception of the Austrian coverage. Fifty years later, the veteran broadcaster György Szepesi recorded an as-live commentary for DVD which was released to critical acclaim in Hungary.

At the time there had been no mention of Puskás scoring four goals anywhere in the Hungarian media except in the Budapest edition of *Népsport* which simply said: 'Real win fifth consecutive European Cup; Real Madrid 7 Eintracht Frankfurt 3; goals: Puskás 4, Di Stefano 3'.

As Hampden glowed in the brilliance of the all-white Madrid, it was impossible not to appreciate that this glamorous side was underpinned by players of serious substance. Puskás was strong, forceful. He could not, would not be bullied.

Puskás and the Real of 1960 had changed football for ever.

PUSKÁS OF SPAIN

Eight years after defeat in the World Cup final of 1954, Puskás was back at the tournament. This time he was playing for Spain. In 1958, as their former captain began his new life in Madrid, Hungary had failed to qualify from their group in Sweden. Despite retaining several players from the *Aranycsapat* era, including Grosics, Bozsik, Sándor and Hidegkuti, they lost 1-0 to Wales in a play-off, having tied for second place.

Four years on, Puskás was recruited for the Spanish national team, under the Italian coach Helenio Herrera. He was 35, and had finished the 1961-62 season with a hat-trick in the European Cup final, as Madrid lost their crown in a 5-3 defeat to Benfica.

It was not uncommon for players to represent a second – or even a third – national team during their career, and alongside Puskás was Di Stéfano, also now 35 and once of Argentina.

Puskás' Spain career would last for four games – one qualifier in Morocco and three group games in Chile. Incredibly for a player who often averaged a goal per game over the course of a season, he did not score a single goal in these matches.

Although they exited the competition early, it is clear that Spain could have been contenders in Chile. They dropped out of their brutal group after a win against Mexico and two single-goal defeats by both eventual finalists, Czechoslovakia and Brazil. They led the eventual champions and World Cup holders by a goal with 18 minutes left in their final group game, and had been 0-0 with the Czechs with 10 minutes to play in their opener.

According to Puskás, the transition from the dominant, attacking tactics which the core of Madrid and Barcelona players were acquainted with, to Herrera's defensive strategy, handicapped them greatly.

"We were used to it at Real Madrid," said Öcsi. "I mean, constantly attacking against every team and of course at one time the Hungarian national team had the same tactics. If we conceded goals at the back we would score more at the front, for sure. But Herrera ordered the team back to defend. We didn't know how to play like that."

Herrera was the coach against whom Czibor schemed with all his effort to oust from Barcelona. According to the Hungarian outside-left "he understood as much about football as a pig does about the calculation of interest".

Herrera became famous in the 1960s as the head coach of Internazionale. He won two European Cups with *Grande Inter* and was in charge when they were defeated by Celtic in the final of 1967. His professional innovation was perfecting the legendary *catenaccio* (bolt-fastener) tactic; the unbreakable Italian defensive system. He employed experimental tactics based on the same idea with Puskás and his Spanish team-mates, but without much success.

Puskás, a naturalised Spanish citizen, was a BBC radio programme guest prior to the Chile World Cup. To the question of how his country's team would perform, he began to describe how the members of the new generation, Flórián Albert, Kálmán Mészöly and Ferenc Sipos would make a great side along with the experienced heads of Gyula Grosics, Károly Sándor and Lajos Tichy.

The reporter asked how he could speak with such love about the country which had driven him away. Puskás made it known that if the reporter was expecting him to speak against his homeland, he would leave the studio. His appearance in the Spanish national team, meanwhile, came with one condition: however it may occur, he would not be willing to play against Hungary. Had Spain finished second in their group, the two nations would have met in the quarter-finals, as Hungary won their group ahead of England, Argentina and Bulgaria.

Puskás stayed on a couple of days after the Spain party returned home, to support his old Hungarian friends – they lost in the quarter-finals to Czechoslovakia – and to catch up with his old friend and neighbour Cucu Bozsik, who was already part of the coaching staff.

THE SPY

HIS NAME was Gyula Pollák, but everybody called him Ali. The best way to describe him is as Puskás' secretary. Ali survived the war but at a tragic cost – his wife and daughter were taken away to a concentration camp and killed. He remained alone for the rest of his life. He found a new family among Hungarian footballers and primarily with Puskás. He was both a fan and friend of Öcsi, who loved him dearly because of his constant good mood.

Ali's task as secretary in the 1950s was primarily to distribute the goods smuggled in from the West – to pass them on. Perhaps they even first got to know each other through this business, or perhaps through the Rosemary Café on Andrássy út, where the fences would meet with the footballers and where, until 1954, Puskás would go every day while he lived on nearby Rökk Szilárd utca.

Ali was already close to Puskás in the 1950s but at that time he didn't live with the family. Nevertheless, when he lost his way during the night he would search for shelter on the roofed terrace of the Puskás residence on Columbus utca and fall asleep there. After 1956, Ali also chose to escape Hungary, and from his letters it comes to light that from time to time he was out of his mind with homesickness. He "couldn't find a partner anywhere to compare with the Hungarian girls".

In Madrid, Ali Pollák became 'Señor Ali' and lived with the Puskás family in their Madrid flat. Puskás' daughter Anikó called him *dadus* – meaning 'nanny' – as Ali was a sort of childminder, taking her to the circus and the zoo and often playing with and looking after her. Ali once took Anikó with him to the famous Chicote cocktail bar on Madrid's Gran Via, where he was a regular.

Ali may well have spied on Öcsi for the Hungarian secret services. In the 1970s their friendship broke down, Ali moved away and, as befits a stateless migrant of the world, he died 10,000 metres above the earth during an aeroplane flight.

"I would never have thought that he was an informer – it is shocking to hear something like this," said József Tóth-Zele, Puskás' former Hungary team-mate and himself another Madrid emigrant, many years later. "He left some of his stuff with me when he went away actually, saying he'd come soon to pick it up – perhaps it's still here somewhere…"

FROM MURCIA
TO MELBOURNE

PUSKÁS – the player who had appeared to be at the end of his career shortly after he turned 30 – did everything he could to extend his playing days. He focused on training, rest and diet and in 1966, aged 39, he was a European Cup winner for the third time, although despite five goals during the earlier rounds, he did not play in the final.

When it was over, it hurt.

"It shattered him that he couldn't play football," said Erzsébet. "It was a difficult period in his life. I'm not saying that he stayed out, or drank too much at the time, but he couldn't find his place and he tried to console himself in his increased free time during evenings spent with his friends. He started to put on weight then, too. It was a big trauma for him.

"Afterwards, when he got a coaching contract and could work again, everything changed. He could go back on the pitch and feel good again. Yes, it was certain that he'd be a coach."

He was in demand immediately, and this would always be the way of it, although the calls would come from far and wide, and not from the calibre of teams who once attempted to recruit him as a player.

According to Spanish regulations, coaches had to complete

a two-year course to work professionally. Puskás, of course, was an exception. When he left football in 1967 he received an offer from the second division team Deportivo Alavés and the association gave special permission for him to start, for the time being without his papers, and to study while he worked.

At coaching school, the practical classes were led by László Kubala – his friend and one-time team-mate. Sándor Kocsis and József Tóth-Zele were among his classmates. The Hungarian friends would make fun of each other. Kubala, as teacher, spoke in Spanish to the Hungarian students when in the presence of the others, addressing them formally. When the time came for practical tasks, Kubala would take his time, then in an impassive voice give the instruction: "Mr Puskás will sprint down the right wing then cross the ball in with his right." In this, of course, he hit Puskás twice: firstly, the sprinting and secondly the right-footed cross (Puskás was notoriously one-footed). He carried out the task perfectly for Kubala, then on his way back up the pitch would swear at him in Hungarian, roughly translated as: "Get to fuck."

Puskás spent 16 months at Alavés, and would only use his Spanish diploma in one other job.

In the 1974-75 season he managed the last-placed team in the first division, Murcia, for four months. Puskás arrived in January, mid-season, shortly after which he answered a journalist's question "What can be done?" with the reply: "We need to sign 16 new players."

His studies were broken by a trip to North America – Puskás would only complete his Spanish coaching qualification upon his return. In the late 1960s, the North American Soccer League (NASL) was making its famous push to break the sport in the USA and Canada, paying big money to some of the most famous names in the game.

Puskás was running his increasingly popular restaurant in Madrid when the offer came. In San Francisco, Golden Gate Gales were looking for a coach and wanted to appoint Puskás as technical director. However, by the end of negotiations, the rich-but-poorly-supported Gales merged with the cash-strapped-but-popular Canadian team Vancouver Royals and relocated to British Columbia. Puskás couldn't resist the lure of football but said later it was a mistake to sell the restaurant and move his family across the Atlantic.

He left for Canada in the summer of 1967. The Puskás family took their then 15-year-old daughter Anikó with them and rented a flat in downtown Vancouver. Puskás was offered $90,000 for three years, but the league went into financial meltdown 12 months later.

Sir Bobby Robson was an unlikely rival for Puskás in Canada, although from the telegram Robson sent Puskás for his 75th birthday in 2002 it is impossible to detect any ill will between the men. Instead, it was a legacy of the merger of the two NASL clubs. Management on the San Francisco side preferred Puskás to take charge of the merged club, while Robson was the choice of the Vancouver contingent. The Americans won out, Robson declined a junior role in partnership with Puskás, and he returned to England.

The Canadians, sympathetic towards Robson, were never at peace with the decision and, according to József Csabai, who coached under Puskás, the English players often sabotaged and undermined Puskás, who was supported by the small French contingent.

Puskás and Csabai – who as a PE teacher in New York had taught the son of John F Kennedy – only came to know the real circumstances of American soccer when they arrived there. In Canada, for example, aside from the stadium they used on matchdays, they could find hardly any pitches. When they were shown the area outside town beside the airport where it was possible to train, they discovered there were no goalposts. The Hungarian coaching pair tried to forge a team, recruiting players of 14 different nationalities from leagues across Europe and the Americas, and taking them to a training camp in Spain. However, at the end of the first championship season there was no more money to cover the long journeys or to run the league. The Puskás family's temporary plans of settling in Canada also faded. In 1968 they returned to Madrid.

Csabai remained, met his wife and raised a family there. The outstanding football coach, physical trainer and chiropractor still lives and works in Vancouver today. He runs a football school and worked for a few years in Europe, where he treated the great Milan team of Gullit, Van Basten, Baresi and Rijkaard.

'I have Ferenc Puskás beside me. What about him?'

"We had already won the league and had agreed with our then coach that he would stay for the following season," says Kitsos Mihalis, the former president of Panathinaikos. "The following day an acquaintance told me that our coach had signed up with the Greek national team. I protested to the state secretary for sport. 'What's this? You take away our coach like this?'

"He explained to me that the national team came first and Panathinaikos only after that. We were unexpectedly left without a coach. I looked up one of my acquaintances who had a travel agency and he had a contact at Real Madrid. He knew the general secretary Augustín Domínguez. We went into the clubhouse and called Real."

Panathinaikos wanted José Santamaría, Real's outstanding former player, but he would not leave as he was the Spain under-21 coach. Dominguez told Mihalis: "I have Ferenc Puskás beside me, though. What about him?"

"I asked back: 'Puskás coaches?' I received the answer, that yes, he did. I said of course we'd be happy to speak to him, he should come over and we'll meet. This is how it happened. I sent the tickets, Puskás arrived and I went out to the airport to meet him, and we came into the town. This was a great sensation in the newspapers – such a famous man hadn't been here before. We went to the clubhouse and agreed everything. He'd get a flat, a monthly salary, a bonus for the Greek cup, another for the championship. The bonus for appearing in the European Cup came up as a last point."

I don't know which of Puskás' senses leapt into life when he insisted during the negotiations with Panathinaikos that they should work out a bonus system in the event of a good European Cup run. It was practically comical that he stipulated such a clause, since it seemed unimaginable that a semi-pro Greek team should make it past the first couple of rounds of the knockout tournament. But Puskás met the directors of the Greek champions, and agreed with them that if Panathinaikos reached the last 16 then he would get so much, then so much if they get to the last eight, and so on. It was not a clause his prospective employers had considered, and they were a little bewildered, but Puskás insisted. They should establish in the contract too, how much he should get if they get to the final.

"If we get to the final, half of Greece will be yours," Mihalis told him.

Puskás took Panathinaikos past Red Star Belgrade, Everton and Slovan Bratislava, holders of the European Cup Winners' Cup, all the way to the final of the European Cup in 1971, and a date with Johan Cruyff's Ajax, who would win the first of their hat-trick of continental titles. Ajax came into the final at Wembley with considerably more experience than Puskás' men, having reached that stage in 1969, when they lost to AC Milan. They also had 24-year-old Cruyff at the peak of his powers, plus Dutch internationals Gerrie Mühren and Johan Neeskens. Ajax took an early lead when Dick Van Dijk headed in a Piet Keizer cross. Thereafter, the Dutch could not make their domination pay and it took until the 87th minute for them to seal victory. Cruyff was the architect, picking the ball up on the right-hand side and flicking a delightful pass into the path of Arie Hann. His shot deflected over Ikonomopoulos and nestled in the net.

This was the start of the great Ajax era – but also a high mark for Greek club football that has never been matched.

This was a team made up of semi-professionals, workers and students. Puskás complemented and encouraged the family atmosphere.

"In those years we spent more time together with Puskás than we did with our families," said Nikos Sakoulis, the interpreter and masseur.

"We earned pennies," said Doctor Frangiskos Sourpis, the centre-back in the European Cup final who later earned a medical degree. "As a medical student, I managed to buy third-hand, a much-used car and English language books from the money earned from the European Cup run, something other students in a similar position possibly wouldn't have been able to do. Football didn't mean that much money, but the club secured work places for the players, or helped in our careers. Whoever had a business among us or earned money from something could organise more and more business thanks to their fame, but they didn't earn much money from football. Nevertheless, we were such a good team.

"Not long ago, we came together on the anniversary and

watched the film of the European Cup final against Ajax. I still say we didn't deserve to lose. On the other hand, we were totally amateur. The team was made up only of Greek players. Still, after 34 years we are very good friends.

"In Greek sport a misconception reigned that we couldn't compete with foreigners, but Puskás said that whoever the opponents were, they had 11, just like we did. He said to me before the European Cup final: 'You take Cruyff – it'll be one of the most pleasant afternoons of your life.'"

Dr Sourpis remembered other Puskás traits. "His name counted for a lot with the referee. It is noticeable in some matches that the referees favour the bigger, more famous teams. With our coach being Puskás, we weren't at any disadvantage.

"Before big matches against intimidating opponents he would calm us down. 'Guys, be relaxed, think about it, today will be one of the most beautiful days in your life. Let's be happy for this opportunity.'

"He didn't keep any kind of distance. He didn't feel he was a world star, yet we were only average players.

"He was a fantastic player. During training he would score repeatedly against us. He warmed-up and enjoyed it. Our keeper hardly improved, since out of 100 shots he'd score 100 goals. We implored Puskás to allow the keeper to save a few shots, as if it carried on then he would let in everything in the match the next day.

"We also went to Spain twice to prepare for our matches. Real received us as guests, naturally because of Puskás. If Puskás stopped to speak with someone at the side of the road, the traffic would stop after a couple of seconds.

"There's something else. There was a basketball court beside our pitch. He lifted the ball into the basket – with his feet. From 10 attempts he scored five baskets. It was unbelievable! "There was also a match between Greece and Italy. The next day the players were talking about how Luigi Riva hit the woodwork with a fantastic free-kick. Puskás heard this and asked for a ball. He put it exactly where the ball was at the free-kick in the previous day's match, and it hit the woodwork in exactly the same place. The players waved their hands, saying he was just lucky. He once more put the ball down at the same spot and again hit the woodwork where he had before. 'Did Riva do it like this?' he asked.

"But he was butter-fingered. This is how we say it in Greece, he didn't take care of his money. He frittered it away, he helped everyone. He was astonishingly generous."

Mihalis, the former club president, has another story. "He gave a lot to Panathinaikos and also received much from the club, but I'm not thinking about finances. An example of how much he worked – not just for money – is that Juan Ramón Verón [father of Juan Sebastián Verón] was available for free. We sent the tickets and Verón arrived, but we didn't know him well enough. I said to Puskás that he should have a look at what we could do with him. He answered that we couldn't condemn such a player to being a trialist. Then at least the doctors should examine him, I thought. They took him to a hospital and examined him there, and the answer arrived that his left leg was two centimetres shorter than his right. As president, I was alarmed. I didn't want to decide on the matter alone, and the management came together. I said to Pancho that I'm going to ask that we don't sign this player. Puskás asked: 'Can I come to the management meeting too?' I naturally said he could.

"'How much can we pay this player?' Puskás asked.

"'1.2m drachmas'.

"To which Pancho said: 'We have to sign him. If he doesn't live up to expectations then take this amount out of my salary.

Bring the paperwork and I'll sign it.' Verón became our best player."

Mihalis, too, explained the Puskás aura in the dressing room. "The secret of Puskás' success was that of the 15 or 16 decent players available to him, he formed a team with a cohesive family atmosphere.

"I remember that we went to play a friendly match against Real in the Bernabéu. When the players first stepped out on to the pitch, 100,000 people were there and they could hardly move from awe.

"Puskás spoke to all the players separately. To the right-back, who was playing against Gento, he said: 'You'll always be on the right, Gento can only use his right foot for walking, he doesn't use it for anything else, just watch his left.'

"But he explained in detail to everyone what they should count on, what their task was. The game finished 1-1. We were ants compared to what he was capable of."

Spilios Sofianopoulos, the former technical director of Panathinaikos, was reputedly a very rich man. He perhaps isn't any more, but he hasn't lost his good humour or his appetite.

"Puskás was born a prince," he said. "He was elegant, generous and intelligent. I was the team's general manager, but he was the boss. It was an honour to work with him.

"I remember after a defeat in Belgrade, when we stood practically no chance of going through, he said: 'If God sleeps in for a bit, perhaps we can go through.' He must have slept in, because we won 3-0 and went through.

"I also personally experienced his fantastic popularity in Spain, when we went to Madrid on his invitation. We visited, ate, drank, went to a match, and when we arrived and they announced Ferenc's name, King Juan Carlos himself came to our box to greet him. Puskás is a 24-carat diamond."

Marsellos Mimis was a restaurateur who worked himself up from nothing after the war to open a restaurant of high repute in Athens. It was his good luck that the restaurant became Puskás' local. When Öcsi returned to Greece for a short spell at AEK Athens in the late 70s, he dined there every night with his wife. A series of celebrities came only so they could stop for a couple of minutes at Puskás' table for a brief conversation.

'Mimi' ran such a fashionable kitchen that when the King of Greece was on holiday abroad he ordered roast piglet from Mimi, which he would have delivered by charter plane to the royal table so he could consume it fresh.

During the 1978-79 season, with the league won, Puskás was sacked with two weeks remaining, apparently so that AEK could avoid paying a bonus for winning the championship. Puskás' Greek friends took AEK to court and won the case. They were awarded around $10,000, at which point Puskás said: "Give it to Mimi, he's building something now and needs the money."

Mimis and Sakoulis were among the first to visit Puskás when he moved into hospital.

Before his return to Greece, Puskás helped to initiate the organisation of professional football in Saudi Arabia. Three former Real superstars – Alfredo Di Stéfano, Héctor Rial and Puskás – received the offer from the Saudi embassy in Spain and were asked to jointly take on the task of national coach. Di Stéfano declined in the end, but Rial and Puskás, who were good friends, took on the assignment. As Puskás recalled: "I thought that it would be a cabaret in the desert." It lasted only a little longer than that – the curtain came down within a year.

During 10 years in Madrid, Puskás studied the language and the customs and soon was able to travel throughout the

Spanish-speaking world and always feel at home – especially in South America.

His next stop was Chile, where he coached that country's most famous club, Colo-Colo, in the mid-1970s, during the reign of the bloody-handed dictator Augusto Pinochet.

He also spent two short periods coaching in Paraguay during the 1980s, firstly with Sol de América, and in the following year, Cerro Porteño.

His employment in Egypt was motivated more by his taste for adventure than any professional calling. His team, Al Masry, were based in Port-Said. Puskás worked there between 1979 and 1985, with two small breaks. His team hovered between third and fifth place, never getting the better of the two dominant clubs in the league, subsidised by the army (El Zamalek) and the state security department (El Ahly). At least in that regard, there was an echo of his distant past in Hungary.

Puskás was 62 and living in semi-retirement when he accepted an offer to coach South Melbourne in Australia. The family sold their Madrid flat, which they had owned for 31 years, and moved across the world again.

In the first year of his contract he won the Australian Cup and in the second year the Australian championship. In the end it took something very special for him to leave this new life. When Puskás left Melbourne, in 1991, it was to finally go back home, to Hungary.

THE EXILE RETURNS

IN the midst of his five-continent tour as a coach, which began at the end of his playing career in the mid-1960s and lasted until the very end of the 1980s, Puskás was given an unexpected opportunity to return to Hungary. In 1981, with the Iron Curtain still in place, neither Puskás nor the government who allowed the exile to return seemed entirely confident in the venture, but this was the beginning of a repatriation process that would see the national hero home for good 10 years later.

During his decades of exile much changed in Hungary. More and more politicians rose to the top who didn't have to bear responsibility for the defection of Puskás all those years ago, or need to vilify him to legitimise the regime. By allowing him to enter and leave the country without trouble, Hungary showed the world it had democracy and freedom. The regime, using more and more credit from Western banks, needed international PR.

Puskás' fears had also receded. The 25 years that had passed since his defection made obsolete the charge against him and eased his own anger against those who had forced him out of the country. In Hungary the government announced: "It is possible to slowly but surely rehabilitate Puskás."

They allowed György Szepesi, who was then chairman of the Hungarian FA, to organise a veterans' match before Hungary's World Cup qualifier against England. Puskás, would once again play on Hungarian soil.

As part of the softening process, András Surányi, a film maker, received a permit and a budget for the making of his documentary film *Aranycsapat*. The film contained contributions from Di Stéfano and Billy Wright. It would serve as a prelude to Puskás' homecoming. During the film's production, Puskás was persuaded to take part and everything fell into place.

The old boys' match took place before the England game, and Puskás travelled directly from the 1981 European Cup final in Paris – where Madrid lost to Liverpool – to Budapest.

On the plane, both Puskás and his wife were uneasy. Erzsébet did not want Öcsi to go the Honvéd match in the afternoon since she was worried about the reaction of the supporters. But when they arrived at the airport they were met by thousands of people celebrating the return of a hero.

The press did not quite know what to do. Puskás' arrival was reported exclusively by those media closest to the government who had planned the event.

The old boys' match was screened live on television, but the broadcaster made no comment on the return of Puskás and treated his presence as if it were normal. They didn't say a word about him being on Hungarian soil for the first time in a quarter of a century.

The match, though, caused a sensation throughout the country. Everyone spoke about Puskás and within minutes it had spread across Budapest that Öcsi had come home. Puskás, of course, scored a hat-trick.

After ending his exile in 1981, he visited Hungary regularly, but still worked in North Africa and Australia. Another 10 years passed until he and his wife fully repatriated. The Hungarian government elected in 1990, following the first free vote since the communists took power in 1948, played a role in tempting Öcsi home, but his decision wasn't easy. For one, he had a contract with Melbourne, he lived and worked in tranquil and beautiful surroundings, was successful, popular and earned well. The second, more important argument against going home was that his family – Anikó and the grandchildren – lived in Spain. They planned to live both in Spain and in Hungary but illness soon made this impossible. The decision, in the end, was an emotional one. Wherever he had been, he played Hungarian cards, loved gypsy music in small bars, and thought of the cemetery where his parents rest.

"These texts were ready when you didn't want to speak to me," says Jack London's hero in the book *Martin Eden*, when he discovers that people are publishing, translating and honouring him with riches, when earlier his work went unnoticed. Puskás could have felt the same in the 1990s and the first decade of the new century, when the decorations arrived on a conveyor belt and were often received from the same people who had frowned upon hearing his name.

On the anniversary of the 6-3 match he received, along with his team-mates, the Order of the Middle Cross of the Republic, the highest Hungarian state decoration possible. On his 70th birthday, in 1997, there was not enough time in which to fit in all the honours bestowed upon him. On that day, the International Olympic Committee president personally brought the Olympic Order to him in Budapest. He received the medal of the President of the Republic and a large-scale gala, broadcast live on television, was organised in his honour in the Budapest Kongresszusi Központ, where the head of the government and the president of UEFA were also present. With no time left that day, the Minister of Defence only got a slot the following day to hand over the sword of honour and confirm his promotion to Colonel.

MANAGER OF HUNGARY

FERENC PUSKÁS was living in Hungary again and hadn't coached since he left Australia. It was 1993 and he was 66 years old. He received the title of international director at the Hungarian football federation. Imre Jenei, the Transylvanian-Hungarian coach who had led Steaua Bucharest to the 1986 European Cup, was a flop as the Hungary national coach and resigned before the end of the qualifiers for the 1994 World Cup. The chances of qualifying vanished with a 1-0 home defeat against Greece but four qualifiers and two friendly matches still remained. Sándor Barcs, the former Hungarian football federation president and UEFA vice-president, proposed that Puskás should be the national team coach for this period.

There was a danger of Öcsi being emotionally blackmailed. The federation were not looking at what was good for Puskás, but how they could divert attention from their own responsibility for Hungarian football being in such a state. This would be sensational news that would traverse the globe.

Puskás accepted the offer, but he had two conditions: that he would take over the manager's job for the next four matches only, and secondly, that he had to speak to his wife first. A botched announcement included this detail, and some in the press joked that the fate of Hungarian football was now in the hands of Mrs Puskás.

Finally, in the spring of 1993, nearly 50 years after Öcsi Puskás first appeared for the Kispest senior squad, he became the coach of Hungary for four matches.

Dezső Novák is the most successful footballer in the history of the Olympics, with two golds and one bronze medal. He was a pillar of the great Ferencváros team of the 1960s and one of only two coaches in Hungarian football to have led a team into the UEFA Champions League: Ferencváros in 1995-96. In 2004, in a dramatic statement, he admitted that for decades he had written reports for the communist secret service on his Ferencváros team-mates and later about his coaching colleagues.

Novák became Puskás' assistant with the national team and had also seen to the training tasks under Puskás' predecessor, Imre Jenei. Of course, it wasn't the first time he'd met with Öcsi. "We even played against each other in the old days. In a Szombathely–Honvéd reserve match in 1955 at the Üllői Út stadion... and we lost," he recalled.

He added: "Later, when with Ferencváros, I played a lot against Spanish teams, and we met many times. He regularly joined the group and did everything he could to make sure we enjoyed ourselves. I remember an after-match banquet in Zaragoza to which he arrived late and only peeped in the window. He didn't want to come in because he saw that he was late, but someone noticed him and all the Zaragoza management stood up and welcomed him with a round of applause. The mood always livened up in his midst, he radiated joy.

"He also helped me when I was already a coach and I went to watch an opponent. He took me by car to Bilbao from Madrid and gave me everything that I needed for my work. After these previous events we became colleagues with the national team. It was wonderful to work with him. He told you how you had to do things, wittily, in his own style."

During a break in a communications workshop on a UEFA coaching course I chatted with Gábor Márton, the former national team defender who became a champion with Honvéd and was a successful player in France. He played for Hungary against Iceland during Puskás' short tenure as national coach and it ended in an ugly defeat. Márton was sent off following a nasty foul and then made for the referee. Puskás ran onto the pitch in order to hold back Márton. With a few words whispered in his ear ("the ref's an idiot, leave it, I'll deal with it...") he calmed the player down and avoided even bigger trouble.

Márton also told how Puskás' solitary win as national coach came about. I watched the match on TV with my friend Román Lorányi (whose father was a Kispest goalkeeper at the time of Puskás) and afterwards we went out onto the street with a Hungarian flag to celebrate. The next day, armed with a copy of *Nemzeti Sport* I read during mass at school, I waited, bursting with pride, at the airport for the winning team. It perhaps shows how far Hungary had fallen since the days of the *Aranycsapat* that this celebration was not for victory at a World Cup, or even a qualifier, but a friendly – the 1993 international testimonial of the Irish defender David O'Leary.

The Hungarian team won 4-2 in Dublin, despite the Republic of Ireland being 2-0 up at half-time, their goals coming from Roy Keane and Niall Quinn. István Hamar, a Kispest striker given his debut that day by Puskás, scored twice to level the game, then Tibor Balog and Flórián Urbán gave Puskás his solitary win as national coach.

These minor successes became defining experiences, however lamentable, when set against the memories of those who saw

Puskás on the pitch, not on the bench. Everyone was curious about what magic Puskás had transformed his team with during the break. The players disclosed all sorts of things. They did everything they could to satisfy the journalists' curiosity. Now, more than two decades on, Márton told me what the winning tactical instructions were: "Öcsi came into the dressing room and with a touch of disapproval in his voice, said: 'You know how to score too, for fuck's sake.' Afterwards, he turned around sharply and went out. He was right, and we scored four goals in the second half.

"He always stood up for the players. When he wasn't the team coach any more – the federation took him everywhere as a celebrity – he also accompanied us to Japan. On the day following our arrival we had to play against the hosts in a three-way tournament which we won, but because of the long journey and the jetlag we were so tired that we were on our knees. The journalists still wrote only bad things about the team. They didn't dare argue with the old man of course and he even reprimanded them, in his own way: 'Go to hell, you sons of bitches! Perhaps you know better how we should play? Then show it!' Things like that. Of course, the journalists didn't dare utter a sound."

I asked Flórián Urbán what it was like to play in the national team under Puskás. The first thing that came into his head was the Ireland match: "It still gives me goose pimples when the celebration he got in Ireland springs to mind. It was freezing. The whole stadium stood and applauded. Someday, I'd love to see a footballer in Hungary being celebrated the way they celebrated Öcsi Puskás then in Ireland."

However, Puskás' tenure wasn't celebrated. After three defeats and that win in Ireland, he left aged 66 on June 16, 1993, ending a 25-year coaching career, and 50 years in football.

He was named director for youth football in Hungary, but when Puskás began to take the task seriously the federation soon made it understood that he shouldn't have plans that were too ambitious. At the Puskás family flat on Logodi utca I held in my hand the letter which Puskás wrote to the then interior minister in charge of sport, Balázs Horváth, with almost naive honesty and enthusiasm about how youth football was dying out. He made it clear that intervention would entail a lot of money and a nationwide youth football programme. "We are running out of time," Puskás wrote at the beginning of the 1990s.

Ten years passed before the Bozsik Programme began, named after his old friend and team-mate, but a couple of years and a change of government later, that was gone.

"Give me a free hand, five years, and I will sort out Hungarian football," said Puskás. He was only used as a figurehead by the federation, as that organisation slowly but surely assisted Hungarian football in its downward spiral. The task he wanted – to rejuvenate Hungarian football and organise an academy, did not come his way. The Felcsút academy took on the Puskás name six months after his death, undertaking to build a football future from his legacy.

THE GREATEST OF ALL TIME?

When FIFA hosted a vote to find the greatest player of the 20th century, only Pelé, Cruyff, Beckenbauer, Di Stéfano and Maradona were ahead of Puskás. The IFFHS [International Federation of Football History and Statistics] named him as the century's greatest goalscorer on the basis of the goals he scored in first-class matches (511 goals in 533 Hungarian and Spanish top-flight games). For a long time he was the world record-holder in terms of the number of the goals for a national team – 84 goals in 85 games for Hungary. Behind Puskás there are great goalscorers such as Pelé (77 in 92), Sándor Kocsis (75 in 68), Gerd Müller (68 in 62) and Imre Schlosser (59 in 68). In 1999, the Italian newspaper *La Gazzetta dello Sport* concluded that, on the basis of his goals in the national team, Puskás was the greatest goalscorer of the century.

When the Hungarian federation collated and updated the national team statistics before their centenary in 2001, they discovered a match played in Lebanon in 1956 that was official but had never been included in the statistics. The executive committee accepted the match as official and Puskás moved up to 84 goals in 85 international appearances (József Bozsik also benefited by seeing his record number of appearances boosted to 101, a quarter of a century after his death). When all of this was uncovered, the newspaper *Nemzeti Sport* gave the statistical amendment pride of place on the front page. *Ferenc Puskás scores for Hungary!* boomed the headline. The edition sold in record numbers.

Between 1943 and 1956 Puskás won league titles and top goalscorer awards, played in a World Cup final, was an Olympic gold medallist and defeated England 6-3 and 7-1 in matches that became landmarks in international football. If Puskás had stopped playing football at this point then he would still be among the best of all time.

All of this was despite political conditions which prevented him from competing in some of the biggest competitions during his peak years. After his introduction to the first team in 1943, he lost one year's playing time because of the war, without which he'd probably have been a Hungary player earlier than August 1945. Had Hungary entered the World Cup in 1950 (they were part of an Eastern Bloc boycott), or the Olympic football tournament in 1956 (the defending champions withdrew after the outbreak of the revolution), then Puskás could have won even more titles; and if we imagine that the national team hadn't disintegrated in 1956, then the team at the 1958 World Cup would have stood a fair chance of becoming world champions.

After missing over a year during the peak of his career due to the FIFA ban, he built a new career in Spain which merits a place at the top table all by itself. In his second career, which began after he turned 30, he became Spanish champion five times, the Spanish league's top scorer four times, European Cup winner three times, and an Intercontinental champion.

In 1960 Puskás was runner-up for the Golden Ball, the European Footballer of the Year award, despite voters from some communist countries refusing to vote for him on political grounds – including the Hungarian representative. Both the European Cup and the Golden Ball started in season 1955/1956. Had they been around earlier, Honvéd and Puskás would surely have been in contention regularly at the start of the 1950s.

Puskás scored a goal in a World Cup final and an Olympic final. He scored seven goals in just two European Cup finals. Goals link his name to the biggest stadiums of the world from Wembley to the Maracanã.

He won the inaugural Intercontinental Cup final with Real against the South American champions Peñarol. Here his two goals and two assists helped make Real Madrid club football's first world champions.

More than 25 years passed between Puskás' first match in professional football, in Nagyvárad in December 1943, and his official farewell match in Madrid, in May 1969. Puskás played for 15 minutes for Real against Rapid Vienna, two years after his last match for Madrid, and in front of 80,000 spectators. Two days later, also in the Estadio Santiago Bernabéu, the European Cup final between Ajax and AC Milan took place. At this, barely 30,000 people were present.

It is a feature of his career, and an argument that should be used when assessing Puskás' place in the pantheon – not only did he play a pivotal role in so many landmark matches in football history, he scored goals in these, the biggest moments of his career. Often, they were goals fit for such stages.

1952 Olympic final:
Hungary 2-0 Yugoslavia
(one goal and a missed penalty)

1953: Central European International Cup:
Italy 0-3 Hungary
(two goals)

1953:
England 3-6 Hungary
(two goals)

1954:
Hungary 7-1 England
(two goals)

1954 World Cup final:
Hungary 2-3 West Germany
(one goal and one disallowed)

1960 European Cup final:
Real Madrid 7-3 Eintracht Frankfurt
(four goals)

1960 Intercontinental Cup final:
Real Madrid 5-1 Peñarol
(two goals)

1962 European Cup final:
Real Madrid 3-5 Benfica
(three goals)

First among all of these is the strike that some call the 'Goal of the Century' from the 6-3 match in London. Hungary were leading 2-1 when Czibor, who had run across the line of a throw-in to the right to drag the England defence out of position, played an inside pass to Puskás. Öcsi was on the edge of the six-yard box and as Billy Wright, the England captain, moved toward him, he played the most impudent of playground tricks, dragging the ball back with the sole of his left foot as Wright slid by, and then drilling the ball high inside the near post as the defender struggled to his feet. It was a move nobody had seen before.

Ask Puskás who was the greatest and the answer was always the same: József Bozsik. He would say that he was a big admirer of Pelé; that Di Stéfano fascinated him; how he marvelled at Matthews, acknowledged Fritz Walter and later praised Maradona. However, he always ended by saying he'd never seen a player like Bozsik, whom he used to call out to play football with a knock on the wall which separated their family homes.

THE DEATH OF PUSKÁS

ERZSÉBET PUSKÁS still remembers the first signs of the illness that would consume her husband's life. "He got up after his afternoon siesta and didn't know if it was evening or morning. At first he had trouble with arithmetic, and he had always been able to work out complicated sums within moments. He didn't understand. He counted it again and again. It didn't come out." In the mid-90s the illness began its attack. Ferenc Puskás was always sharp-minded, a pun-maker and great conversationalist. As this acute form of cerebral sclerosis did its work, he slowly forgot everything – the languages he had learned, the experiences he had lived through, the friendships he had made, the faces he loved.

Erzsébet remembers: "After we moved into Logodi útca, we went shopping every day. They knew and loved him in the shop across the street and after that he'd go to the takeaway for dinner. Then one evening I waited and waited, but he didn't come home. He'd got lost. Later, it happened again.

"After that, there was the newspaper. I noticed that he looked and looked at it, but wasn't reading. He knew there was something wrong."

Slowly, he lost his ability to communicate. He handled formal situations by falling back on decades of experience, but he was ill long before he was admitted to hospital.

Alfredo Di Stéfano first noticed something awry in Vienna in 2000. "When I asked about water, he gave an answer about wine."

I heard him give a speech at the end of the 1990s, and it was practically impossible to make out anything from it.

He was admitted to hospital in 2000. The family kept the news close.

"He was in the loony bin, as we called it in my day," said his wife. "The surroundings were nicer there, but it still wasn't good for him. They were three to a room. I fretted a lot about what could be done. Many people called from Spain too, saying I should take Öcsi there. I also went around more hospitals here. There are beautiful private hospitals in the countryside, in wonderful surroundings. But how would I have visited him there? Already I couldn't stand it if I didn't see him every day. The Kútvölgyi hospital was close, with a taxi I would be there within minutes. He started there, he got used to the staff. Nevertheless, we didn't plan it that way."

Suddenly the world took note: Ferenc Puskás was seriously ill in hospital. The rumour also spread that he didn't have money for the treatment and was in need of help. In Greece they began to raise funds and Panathinaikos sent a few thousand dollars. Erzsébet had to refute in the foreign papers that her husband needed money. The government also replied quickly – after all, the news was embarrassing for them. The nation's favourite son was being treated in the Kútvölgyi, the old Communist Party hospital. A government spokesman said Puskás would receive whatever he required in the way of treatment.

Later, his former Hungary team-mate Jenő Buzánszky and other family friends ensured Öcsi's room was renovated. He got normal furniture, satellite TV, a comfortable little living space. The football federation, the government and a large Hungarian gas company gave money so that Puskás' room and the neurological department at the Kútvölgyi were made more pleasant. In 2003, the sports minister Ferenc Gyurcsány inaugurated the new room at a hospital press conference. Öcsi was still – albeit with faltering and wavy letters – able to sign a few photos.

Sepp Blatter and Alfredo Di Stéfano came to the hospital, the president of the Spanish FA, and many, many friends, foreign and Hungarian. József Csabai and József Csóka; later Jenő Buzánszky and Gyula Grosics with monthly regularity; the Hungarian football federation president and general secretary Imre Bozóky and Sándor Berzi on every important occasion; friends from Athens and a few lucky supporters also came if they somehow won the trust of the hospital and the family.

There was another faithful visitor. Miklós Fejér, the patron of the old footballers and the owner of the Régi Sipos restaurant in Budapest, brought delicacies. Puskás was always present at the 6-3 anniversaries and his team-mates' birthdays at the restaurant. His birthday celebrations outgrew the restaurant and had to be held in hotels or ballrooms. Four times a year, Miklós invited the staff and carers from the rehab unit – from the doctors to the porter, together with the famous patient – to dinner.

His carer, Jenő Kovacs, became very close to Puskás. If the weather and the state of his patient permitted, he would take Puskás by the arm and knock a ball around. They also went out to the stadium named after Puskás. Control the ball, shoot.

"It's still visible today who he was. When he gets the ball he controls it and sets it up to shoot," Jenö said at the time.

These moments became less frequent, and the days passed

slowly as Puskás' condition worsened. Husband and wife would sit in silence, hand in hand.

Puskás died on Friday November 17, 2006. Parliament broke off its session, stood to attention in respectful silence, each party speaker eulogising Ferenc Puskás. The Prime Minister sent his condolences by letter, the leader of the opposition by telephone and the government announced the day of his funeral, December 9, to be a day of national mourning. The army posthumously promoted Puskás from the rank of colonel to brigadier general.

The funeral took place with a turbulent atmosphere engulfing the country. Violent demonstrations occurred on the 50th anniversary of the 1956 Uprising and the international press was full of news arriving from Budapest of street clashes and police brutality. There was conflict, also, around the funeral. The family had initially planned a discreet, private service, but became aware of an expectation at home and abroad that Puskás' funeral would be of a scale befitting his legend, which would only be possible if the state funded the event. On the other hand, the family had requested that the government should not take ownership of the funeral. As a compromise, the Olympic Committee organised the funeral jointly with the Hungarian football federation, funded by state money.

'Farewell from the nation.' This was the title that the organisers gave to the grand ceremony. On the day before the funeral, his body was laid out in state in the basilica for long lines of Hungarians and foreigners to pay their respects. The ceremony, held at the Puskás Ferenc Stadion, was also geared towards a large public presence. A catafalque[18] was built in the

---

18   a raised box, or similar platform, often movable, that is used to support a coffin

centre circle, all the players from the first- and second-division Hungarian teams arrived to form a ring around the pitch, whilst the public said farewell from the stands. The former and honorary president of the Hungarian FA György Szepesi, who had commentated on Puskás' early career for radio, said his farewells, speaking into a microphone set up at the side of the pitch, as did Real Madrid president Ramón Calderón, who had arrived with a delegation via private jet so that afterwards he could return to Spain in time for Real's league match at Sevilla that evening. Inside Szent István Basilica, the guests included President of the Republic László Sólyom, MLSZ president István Kisteleki, Michel Platini, Franz Beckenbauer and FIFA president Sepp Blatter.

In Belfast, a city with a population of some 270,000, there were more than 100,000 at the roadside as the funeral procession for the great George Best passed by in December 2005. In Budapest, a city of two million, there were approximately 8000 present in the stadium and, at most, 20,000 along Andrássy út. The ceremony itself was beautiful and befitting of the occasion, but the aftershock of the violent demonstrations, and generations worth of propaganda aimed at discrediting Puskás within Hungary played a part in the public reception. Perhaps it had to be thus: Hungary bade farewell to its most famous son in an ambiguous manner.

UEFA posthumously awarded its highest decoration, the UEFA Order of Merit in Emerald, to Puskás. Madrid named a street after him. His statue resides in the president's meeting room in the Estadio Santiago Bernabéu and his bust at the club's Ciudad Real Madrid training complex. In Hungary, there are streets, schools, sports centres and statues dedicated to the country's most famous son. He will never be forgotten.

EPILOGUE

The Hippo

IT is the summer of 1991, somewhere to the south of Sydney, and George Best and Denis Law are preparing to go out on the training fields with a group of youngsters desperate to become professional players.

The great players are pulling on their tracksuits when they hear a muttering from the dressing room next door. Young Australians are taking the mickey out of their coach.

Best hears a boy say: "Do you know what we should do? Let's ask him to run a bit with the ball."

Roars of laughter are followed by an observation from another youngster: "I saw how he went across the pitch this morning – like a hippo. He can't play with a stomach like that. He can hardly get into his tracksuit."

Another burst of loud derision.

Another pointed out: "Yesterday was also a complete waste of time. We don't even understand what he is saying, his English is that bad. I seriously doubt that he was ever a proper football player. He's a fatso."

Law's group was ready for training, but Best had to wait for his players to arrive. He decided to walk around the fields.

He saw a group of youngsters split into two. One team of

boys wasn't even listening to the coach and were kicking the ball about aimlessly.

The coach was trying to explain something without much success. Best described him as "big, bordering on fat, there was more oil on his swept back hair than on a mechanic's rag. His face was saggy and grey, a sharp contrast to the tanned hew of his students. The elastic of his tracksuit trousers was at full stretch due to his large belly."

As Best neared, he was recognised by the boys, prompting a murmur of awe. Best looked at the coach, smiled at him and nodded towards a bag of balls. He called over the rebellious group and set up 10 balls on the turf, 30 yards from goal.

"I'm going to ask your coach to shoot from here and try to hit the bar. How many times do you think he will be successful?" Best asked the players.

One said: "Once! If he's lucky."

The coach trudged over. Best recalled years later: "He glanced up, measured the distance and, nimbly standing on his right leg, with his left he tentatively struck the ball. The parabola was perfect. The ball bounced off the top of the bar with a loud smack. Now that he had measured the distance, he hit the second ball more firmly. The ball was still rising as it hit the bar like a tuning fork. His next eight shots all hit the bar. The boys watched on astounded, jaws gaping.

"I went over to get one of the balls and hit it towards the coach. He chested it down and the ball was instantly under his spell. He played keepie-uppie for about half a minute, effortlessly using left and right before heading off towards the goal. On the way there he kept the ball up with his right foot, on the way back, with his left. The ball never once touched the ground.

"When he got back to us I raised my right hand as if to say, 'carry on as long as you like'. He nodded, carried on for a bit with his right, and then kicked the ball high into the air. He leaned forward, the ball resting between his shoulders. He tensed his neck muscles which made the ball rise into the air once more, and he began playing head tennis. Once he bored of this, he tilted his head back a little and now the ball rested on his forehead for a few seconds. Once again he tensed his neck muscles and the ball flew into the air."

The show went on.

"He kneed the ball, then with the outside of his foot, and then with his heel, continued playing keepie-uppie, before once again sending the ball skyward. 'There's the goal!' – he shouted as the ball came down. Leaning forward, he let fly from a good 30 metres. The shot almost burst the net."

The boys cheered and applauded. They had been confronted with the genius of Ferenc Puskás.